City of Children

Francesco Tonucci

Institute of Cognitive Sciences and Technologies
of the National Research Council, Italy

B|S Bridging Languages and Scholarship

Series in Urban Studies

VERNON PRESS

www.vernonpress.com

In the Americas:
Vernon Press
1000 N West Street,
Suite 1200, Wilmington,
Delaware 19801
United States

In the rest of the world:
Vernon Press
C/Sancti Espiritu 17,
Malaga, 29006
Spain

Series in Urban Studies

Bridging Languages and Scholarship

Library of Congress Control Number: 2019951710

ISBN: 978-1-64889-025-3

Also available: 978-1-62273-763-5 [Hardback]; 978-1-62273-935-6 [PDF, E-book]

Translator: Dessy Vassileva
Copyeditor: Ellisa Anslow
Cover designer: Marianna Pascariello
Production editor: Argiris Legatos

Cover image by Francesco Tonucci.

Copyright © of first edition: Editrice Laterza, Bari, 1996.

This book is a translation of *La Città dei Bambini: Un modo nuovo di pensare la città* (Editrice Laterza, Bari, 1996). This English edition by Vernon Press forms part of the Bridging Language and Scholarship (BLS) initiative and follows previous editions of this important work in Italian, French, Portuguese and the four languages of the Spanish nation (Galego, Basque, Catalan and Castilian); sharing its central message of great importance with the English-speaking world.

To Federico and Nina, my grandchildren,
and to all grandchildren,
because they are our future.

To all of us, grandparents,
because we dedicate the most selfless
and free part of our lives
to build our grandchildren's future.

Table of contents

Appendix

Bibliography

Preface

An Issue with Languages and a Gift

This English version is a gift, a very important gift for which I thank Vernon Press. When I was studying, the foreign language taught at school was French. Back then, in Italy, French was the international language, for example, in diplomacy. It was only decades later, during my son's generation when the world realised that this was no longer true, and that English had taken its place as the new international language. But it was already too late for me. However, being a researcher myself, it seemed that I had no choice but to learn that language, and that is when my long, tiring, and frustrating battle with English started. Sadly, a losing battle. I tried everything: classes, books, tapes, even a month-long stay in Guilford, near London, but it all came to nothing. At some point, to preserve my mental health, I decided to give up, not without bitterness, though. At that point, I was sure that I just wasn't able to learn another language, and I resigned myself to that. After all, French didn't turn out to be particularly useful either. Then, two unpredictable things happened.

In Italy we have many dialects, every city has a different one, which usually varies from area to area. I obviously knew the dialect of my own city and, over time, I started learning the dialect of my wife's city, which at first seemed incomprehensible. For the local people, it was something unique, something that had never happened before. In the same period, my Spanish experience began. I started going to Spain every year for a few days; I used to communicate with people in Italian, and they understood me easily. Then the Spanish language started developing in my mind, without having to force myself to learn it, just as my wife's dialect had. Just as it happens when a child of a few months' old first learns to talk, it comes naturally, as he is surrounded by people who love him and who talk to him in that same way. So, I learned Spanish, which I now use with ease to communicate, give conferences, and do interviews. My defeat suffered at the hands of English, and my victory over Spanish, subsequently guided and influenced my career. After Spain came Latin America, and so my books also came to be published and well-known in these countries. The Anglo-Saxon world was left aside, far away. This is the reason why this edition really is an unexpected gift for me and, due to that, doubly appreciated.

Elizabeth Rahman deserves a mention and a kind thanks as well. This is also a strange story where luckily Spain and England collide. Elizabeth teaches at Oxford University, but we met on the Spanish island of Fuerteventura, where she lives and where I was due to speak at several conferences to present the project "The City of Girls and Boys". We talked about many things, including my difficulty making contact with the Anglo-Saxon world. She set things in motion very efficiently, and a few months later, thanks to her, the meeting with Vernon Press took place. Therefore, if I am the father of this book, Elizabeth is the godmother.

I hope that this edition, besides the personal attachment, will carry the ideas and the philosophy that are behind this project over to the Anglo-Saxon world which, during such a complex and problematic time that our planet finds itself in, proposes a simple but revolutionary solution: make our world, our cities, and our schools suitable for the needs and rights of children. This would solve many problems for us all.

Finally, it seems auspicious that this book will be published in the same year as the 30th anniversary of the approval of the International Convention of Childhood Rights by the United Nations.

Francesco Tonucci
Rome, 20 November 2019

Prologue

First assessment after more than twenty years

Francesco Tonucci
20 November 2014
(25th anniversary of the International Convention of Childhood Rights)

A short story

In May 1991, the City Council of Fano, the city where I was born, organized a week dedicated to children with the name "The city of children", and asked me to act as a consultant in this demonstration. During the week, activities, conferences and exhibitions were planned for, and with, the children, which concluded with the big "The city to play" party on Sunday; for which the main streets were closed to traffic so that the children could play. During that week, an extraordinary municipal plenary session was held in the largest theater in the city with the presence of hundreds of children and some guests; among which was Mario Lodi. The children presented their ideas and proposals and, as a grand finale, the plenary approved an agreement committing to repeat this initiative every year; and to which I was assigned as their scientific manager.

A few days later, I wrote a letter to the city mayor accepting the position, in which I also suggested that instead of considering "The city of children" an annual event, it would become a permanent project of transformation for the city with the boys and girls as its parameter of change. I proposed to the Administration that, for the realization of this project, a laboratory be created, a specific project team to be employed, and that a relevant headquarters be assigned where the team could work and meet other operators also dedicated to childhood and the children directly involved in the various activities. Thus, the project was born which at that time was called "The city of children" and is now, more adequately called "The city of girls and boys." It originated in my city, but since its first years, it has attracted the attention of the public and several Italian cities.

I remember that in the first documents I sent to the mayor I made it clear that the main objective of this project should be to give children the possibility of leaving home unaccompanied, allowing them to have the fundamental experiences of exploration, adventure and play with their friends.

Why in 1991: from being protected to being citizens

In 1991, Italy recognized the Convention on the Rights of the Child, approved by the United Nations in New York on November 20, 1989; Spain had already recognized and assumed it in 1990. The convention put an end to a long journey of our democracies regarding children's rights. The world that emerged from the two world wars was materially and morally destroyed. In the name of absurd ideologies, entire villages were exterminated, cities were destroyed without repairing their architectural and artistic treasures, and a large part of the population was sentenced to starve. World politics observed this long experience of horror and bloodshed in disbelief and humiliation. Cities were full of orphaned children, abandoned, without protection or hope.

On November 20, 1959, the United Nations approved the Declaration of the Rights of the Child: ten principles proclaim children's rights to be defended, protected and cared for against diseases, illiteracy, labor and sexual exploitation, military exploitation in tribal wars and crime. The introduction of a tutelary intervention was necessary and urgent. However, in those years, science was studying child development thoroughly and, first by Freud, then Piaget, Vigotsky and Bruner, childhood was recognized as the most fundamental period of human development. In the nineteen-thirties, Janusz Korczak, the great Polish educator, wrote his Declaration of the Rights of the Child with phrases such as: "The child has the right to live in the present" and "The child has the right to protest an injustice".[1]

On November 20, 1989, the United Nations approved the Convention on the Rights of the Child that confirms the rights to guardianship, defense and protection, which for the first time, formally declares the full citizenship of children from birth. From that moment on, girls and boys are no longer future citizens, adults in training, but citizens and, therefore, holders of rights.

Our project was born and developed with the aim of reminding cities of the duty to put this solemn effort, assumed by all of the countries of the world, into practice and, especially, to recognize the citizenship of children.

Unfortunately, 25 years after its approval, this fundamental law is not yet in the public domain and, perhaps for that reason, it is not applied at large. Moreover, while something is being done to reduce the deficiencies linked to

---

[1] Janusz Korczak (1878–1942) was a doctor, pedagogue and writer. He dedicated his life to orphaned Jewish children in Warsaw organizing the orphanage as a fascinating children's republic. When the Nazis deported the little orphans to the Treblinka extermination camp, Korczak, who could have been saved, wanted to accompany them and on August 6, 1942, he entered the gas chamber with them.

the fundamental rights of children such as life, health, dignity and education, nothing is done to recognize the child as the protagonist of his and our story.

Articles 12, 13 and those following, which recognize the right to freedom of opinion, expression and association, are practically unknown; the right to rest and leisure and to engage in play, stated in article 31, is completely underestimated. And all this because it is preferred that we overlook the fact that article 3 of this convention declares that the interests of the child should always be considered above all else and, therefore, be a priority over those of any other person.

Federico, a ten-year-old member of the City Council of the Boys and Girls of Rome, after his first year of work, told his mayor: " We ask this city for permission to leave home unaccompanied." A strange proposal, as parents are the only ones who can either grant or deny that permission. But Federico knew that, if he asked his parents, they would say that he could not because the city does not allow it, so he approached the mayor and said: "Give me permission."

Federico and his parents surely have a similar opinion about the city, but draw completely different conclusions. The parents say: "The city is dangerous, so you can't leave. If you have to leave, we will accompany you, probably by car". Federico thinks: "The city is dangerous, so you have to change it." His parents have resigned themselves; they consider the state of affairs as something objective, unaffiliated with their will and their power. Federico has not resigned, he needs his autonomy, so he strongly asks for change. It reminds us of St. Augustine's phrase: "Hope has two beautiful daughters. Their names are anger and courage; Anger at the way things are and Courage to see that they do not remain the way they are".

The project was born with, and has developed according to, this goal – to take advantage of the anger and courage of children to change cities.

The international network

As mentioned earlier, the project has been of interest to the public, the media and cities since its inception and a small network of cities was quickly formed; one which recognizes the annual celebration of Fano as its meeting and exchange point. In 1996, the National Research Council, my workplace, took on the project and assigned the management and coordination to me; which was consequently moved from Fano to Rome.[2] From that moment on, the network expanded and, over time, more cities and countries were added. The current network is made up of about two hundred cities in Italy, Spain, Argentina, Uruguay, Colombia, Mexico, Peru, Chile and Lebanon. In the case of Italy and Spain, the project has generally embraced small-medium sized cities, while in Latin America large cities such as Buenos Aires, Rosario, Córdoba and Mar del Plata in Argentina, Bogotá and Medellín in Colombia, Lima in Peru, Montevideo in Uruguay, and Santiago in Chile have done so.

In recent years, national or regional networks have been created to promote the coordination and exchange of experiences between cities. In particular, since 2000, the Educational Action Association of Madrid[3] organizes a national congress every two years with includes all of the Spanish cities that either already form part of the project "The city of children", or that are interested in it. In 2014, the eighth meeting was held. In 2012, the association won the Habitat Award of the United Nations thanks to this experience with the project "The city of children".

Since 2007, at the request of Governor Hermes Binner, the province of Santa Fe has had a Latin American Laboratory, in order to extend the project to the cities of the province of Santa Fe and offer support and coordination to the Argentine and Latin-American cities who have joined this experience.

In 2014, with the support of the University of Deusto and the autonomous administration of the Basque Country, a network was formed in this community.

A book as a toolbox

The project awakens a lot of interest and an increasing number of cities are requesting meetings, conferences, and counsel. I am required to attend hundreds of meetings, which drove me to publish this book in 1996. A book whose purpose is to help cities interested in joining the project, a kind of 'toolbox' that explains the meaning of the offer, its philosophy, and illustrates its operational proposals, with the experience of Fano as a substantial reference, which until then was the first and the most organized. Of course, the effect of the book was just the opposite of that expected by the author and,

---

[2] Currently, the International Laboratory of the project "The city of girls and boys" has been integrated into the Institute of Cognitive Sciences and Technologies of the CNR (www.lacittadei-bambini.org) and is managed by a working group, led by the author, and of which Antonella Prisco and Daniela Renzi are part.
[3] For more information see: *Acción Educativa MRP* – www.accioneducativa-mrp.org

instead of reducing the requests for meetings, trips, and training courses, they increased exponentially and worryingly so to this very day.

Among all my books, this is the only one that has been fortunate to be translated into the four languages of the Spanish Nation with the titles *La ciudad de los niños, La ciutat dels infants, Haurren Hiria,* and *A cidade dos nenos.* There is also an Argentine edition with several reprints and many editions in Italy.

In 2002, it was considered necessary to reflect new ideas, new experiences, and it was believed that an expanded reissue of the first book would not be sufficient. Then, *Se i bambini dicono: Adesso basta!* (When children say: Enough!) was published. This second book was intended to be the continuation and update of "The city of children", but instead of narrating the experiences of different cities, the floor was given to the children. Twenty-six sentences with children's proposals or complaints became the twenty-six chapters of the book. In each of them, the author answers two questions: Why does a child say that? What could be done if children were heard? Thus, a broad analysis of the current child condition and a vast repertoire of the initiatives, activities and experiences carried out in the cities in these years, and other possible ones, emerged to provide concrete answers to the children's expectations.

First assessment after more than twenty years

During the presentations of this project, we are often asked whether we can make an assessment of these over twenty years, and if we can affirm that in the cities that adhered to the project, real changes have been made and verify the nature of them. It is not easy to give an answer. Many projects similar to ours require the increase and improvement of activities and services for children. In these cases, the assessment is simpler if the changes from one initial state to another are considered by measuring the opening hours of the services, the square meters of the green areas, and the spaces available for children. However, in our case, we ask cities for a radical change, almost a complete transformation. That's why we talk about a "New philosophy of city governing". In general, children are not heard, and their ideas are not taken into account as real components of the city's administrative policy. Typically, children are not allowed to go out alone to see their friends, to get to know their environment or experience playing freely.

Offering children these spaces, these opportunities, raises strong conflicts with the interests of adults, politicians, teachers and their parents. The most frequent and significant disputes are against the unlimited power of automobiles, against the disappearance of public spaces, against the occupation of free time with homework and extracurricular activities, against the disinterest shown by adults for children's opinions and needs.

With this premise as a starting point, it seems to us that these are the significant changes observed in the adults' behavior of the cities participating in the project.

More time dedicated to children

In all participating cities, politicians have spent significantly more time on childhood policies; discussing interventions in their favor and talking directly with children. Experiences that have already been practiced, such as visits to schools, have been reinforced and other more authentic experiences, filled with possibilities have been implemented.

Listen to the children

The best channel for the relationship between city politics and children has been the Girls and Boys Council. Young children, chosen by a raffle, periodically meet with an adult to offer the mayor the child's point of view, as stated in article 12 of the convention. City authorities listen to the children and try to address their proposals.

Change of priorities

In the most responsive cities, interventions are often observed in favor of pedestrians and bicycles or of public spaces. However, these points are often overshadowed by those considered urgent and imperative, such as traffic, parking, and roundabouts. In our cities, changing the order of priorities has been accepted on many occasions; favoring pedestrians over cars, neighborhoods over cities, children over adults, and play over work.

The case of Pontevedra

Two years ago, when I returned to Pontevedra and presented myself to the mayor, he said: "Francesco, this is your city." He explained that ten years ago he had attended my presentation on the project "The city of children" and it had convinced him. At that time, he was already the mayor and has since tried to modify the city to correspond with these premises. He cited the exact problem regarding priorities. I had criticized the way in which the issue of urban mobility is addressed by considering the problem of private traffic as a priority and trying to facilitate it. To facilitate urban mobility, the traffic lanes are widened, roundabouts are created, parking lots are increased. The result is that the sidewalks are narrowed, making it more complicated and dangerous to travel on foot.

He proposed to reverse the priorities: starting with the problems of pedestrians, then cyclists, public means of transport and, finally, private means. In Pontevedra, a nine-meter street dedicated six meters to cars, while for pedestrians and street furniture (street lamps, bins, benches) there were two sidewalks of a meter and a half. Pedestrians had to go in a single file and, if they carried a stroller or a wheelchair, it was impossible. They have reversed the priorities, first examining the needs of pedestrians, and have decided that two people with an open umbrella should be able to pass each other on a sidewalk (it rains a lot in Pontevedra). As a result, each sidewalk is two and a half meters wide and, with the furniture, three meters. There are three meters left for cars – the streets are one way and there are no parking spaces. The other problem I had raised was the right of pedestrians to have a continuous march, without interruptions or level changes (think of the people in a wheelchair). Today, in Pontevedra, all pedestrian crossings are at the height of the sidewalks and it is the cars that must go up and down. In Pontevedra, the maximum speed in the entire city is 30 km/h and in the historic center 20 km/h. Two years ago, the City Council invited all children over the age of six to go to school on foot and without adults to accompany them.

A democratic election

Choosing pedestrians over cars means siding with everyone instead of some, because we are all pedestrians, and being pedestrians is the only thing we have in common. Some use private means, others public, others cycle, but all, at some point are pedestrians. Choosing the small city instead of the big one is also a democratic choice – we all live in a neighborhood and many of its inhabitants do not leave. Therefore, it is fair to invest, as a priority, in projects and resources in the small city of the neighborhoods that guarantee the highest possible quality of life for all citizens; from the smallest and most vulnerable.

Increased autonomy of movement

Many of our cities have embarked on a complicated but honest process to reverse the seemingly unstoppable tendency to limit the autonomy of movement of girls and boys in their own city. In some cities, thousands of children, aged six and above, take the route between their home and school every day without adults. They go with their friends instead, who they then meet up with in the afternoon to play. In all these years, children from various countries and cities of different dimensions and social characteristics have shown that they know how to move with responsibility and caution.

A new security policy

The Girls and Boys Council of Rosario, a large Argentine city where children are in real danger of aggression and kidnapping, has claimed, however, their right to autonomy. The question of how this objective could be achieved, elicited several conventional proposals such as: "more police", "more control from the adults", "surveillance cameras in the streets"; all of which repeated what they had heard from parents, from teachers and on TV. One of the smallest children even suggested: "Adults should help us, but from a distance". An original, unpredictable proposal that demands a change: adults should not behave as parents only to their own children, but as citizens; creating security, concern, solidarity. Faced with the traditional political proposals of reaching higher levels of security by increasing defensive instruments, which are very expensive and ineffective, children instead propose the policy of the presence, of the occupation of public space, of people's interest in the public space and safety, starting with that of the children. I remember, with excitement, in Mexico City, perhaps one of the most complex cities in this regard, when the mayor, after hearing my proposal, affirmed before the children, politicians and the media that, in his opinion, this was the authentic revolution –restoring the children's autonomy, allowing them to be safe again in their neighborhoods.

A diverse way of doing politics

Hermes Binner, who was the first mayor of Rosario and later governor of the province of Santa Fe, often repeats that he has learned to do politics through "The city of girls and boys" project. What it has taught him is that political decisions, if intended to be correct and effective, must always be transversal and include all the competencies of the Administration. Therefore, we maintain that this is a project of the mayor, of the city, and not one of its sectors or competencies.

Interest in scientific research

The International Laboratory, in line with the objectives of our public research body, has developed study programs in recent years to analyze the effects of the activities proposed by the project; as much as on children who have participated in it, as on adults and the social environment. Other research organizations and several universities in the cities of the network have participated in this activity.

The need for a new edition

Books have a life, they are written, published, they are often well received and successful, then they lose their strength and presence. It is difficult to find them in bookstores and, finally, they are sold out and disappear. This book has had a long and fruitful life, many translations and editions. But, apparently, the project it proposes has a longer life. This is the reason why, once the first edition was sold out and faced with the requests of interested people and new cities joining the project, I thought to give it a new lease of life. I hope that the book continues to accompany the administrators, teachers, and parents interested in this new philosophy of city governing.

Foreword

Dear Frato,

I was very pleased to receive the drafts of your book. I read them right away because you write with simplicity: clear, accessible, like a polite and kind person who loves his readers and helps them understand the text effortlessly, with correct arguments, with unpretentious, every-day language, with examples that everyone can understand and that, like the ones you offer, are part of the experiences of each and every one of us. I was immediately attracted to the beautiful image, which is shown at the beginning, according to which the city today becomes the forest from the tales for children. Not too long ago, the children were afraid of the forest, where wolves and evil witches lived, while they felt safe in the city. Now things have been reversed, the city has become hostile: "gray, aggressive, dangerous, monstrous." The book is permanent praise to the fantasy, creativity, freedom, intelligence, spontaneity, extraordinary wealth of ideas and feelings, typical of the world of children.

For me too, not only for the children, the city is hell. But I protect by leaving home less and less. My life can pass in the four walls of my study without too many inconveniences. But I have not forgotten my life as a child. On the contrary, it reappears with increasing clarity in my memory. The most beautiful memories of my childhood are those of holidays in the country, when we played in the open air without any danger and wandered along the paths, where occasionally an ox-drawn carriage passed by.

But also, my city was totally different. We lived in Turin in a neighborhood of recent construction, in a "stately" home, as they said then, on the corner of a cut street, which ended shortly after our gate. It was called Gasómetro Street (today it has changed its name), because the neighborhood had been built where the old building, already non-existent at that time, that supplied heat and light to the city (the streetlights of my childhood streets were still gas-powered) was.

It was enough to go down the stairs to reach our "game room." There was no danger. We were going down alone. We didn't play on the road, because it was paved. We played on the sidewalk. Our games were "sidewalk" games. And now, in the city, those games have disappeared.

Among them the spinning top, which the most courageous took in their hands while still turning and threw it against the top of its adversary to knock it down; the marbles made to slide with a blow of the index finger and the thumb. The "week" (similar to Hopscotch), a more feminine game, to tell the truth, that consisted of jumping on one foot on a rectangular outline drawn with chalk, where each box represented a day and the first to arrive on Sunday without falling won. The "stamps", as the stickers torn from the matchboxes were called and which, once placed one on top of another forming a small tower, were struck from a distance with a flat stone making it slide down the sidewalk and the winner was the one who made the most stickers fall.

A few years later, when we were in high school, a group of five or six of us who lived in the same area returned from school. We walked along a long ,straight, deserted street (today it has become almost impassable because of so many cars parked on either side, some even in double-parked), so deserted that we were advancing kicking a ball, as if we were the strikers of a soccer team, until the moment in which we separated and each one took the path to his house. At that point, there was a church which was always closed, whose doorway served as a goal for our last strikes.

We also played in the yards. I spent hours on the kitchen balcony watching the children in the adjoining houses, who played hide and seek, chase, four corners, cops and robbers. It was almost as if I was playing with them – I learned new games, which I practiced with my friends in the small courtyard of our house, in which the doorwoman's son was the king; he was much more skilled than I was in all games.

Nowadays the space in the yards has been reduced more and more. Why reduced? Once again, due to the cars, which have pushed the inhabitants of the houses to each build their own garage. My children have never played in the yard. And the worst part is that the "elders" have begun to complain about the fuss that children make with their screaming and have forbidden them to play in the afternoon when they return from school. They do not complain, however, about the noise that cars make when leaving the garage in the morning and when they return in the afternoon.

It's true, the children have disappeared from the city. They are found only in the parks where their games are the usual: the slide and the ring. I live on a long street with courtyards where children could play without any danger. But it is clear that this practice has been lost. The courtyards have been built not for children to play, but instead in favor of vendors. The porches are, like pedestrian areas, a space for shops and, if any, for the elderly, who can walk more freely, when window shopping. Children are only interested in toyshops and the odd pet store, such as the one below my house, which is an obligatory stop for my grandchildren when they come to visit their grandfather.

I don't know why I have told you these things. It has been a way of expressing my sympathy for your ideal city.

Norberto Bobbio

Warning and gratitude

The "Bibliography", the interviews in the files 20, 21, 22 and 23 of the third part and the data in file 9 were the work of Antonella Rissotto, collaborator of the Institute of Psychology of the CNR (National Research Council).

To my colleagues Vito Consoli and Antonella Rissotto, I thank you for the reading and corrections of the different versions of this book.

I thank the mayors of Fano and the advisors who liked and defended the Laboratory, Beatrice Della Santa and Gabriella Peroni, who gave form and reality to the ideas developed together; Paola Stolfa, Giovanna Mancini and Ippolito Lamedica, who, as architects and urban planners, elevated the ideas of the Laboratory, encouraging the groups of children in the project; Alfredo Pacassoni, who shared the birth of the project and its first steps.

To the mayor and the City commission government of Palermo, I thank you for believing in this project and wanting to consider it as a challenge for the future of their city.

I thank for their collaboration in the interviews, Fiorenzo Alfieri, Pilar Figueras, Raymond Lorenzo, Dario Manuetti and Carlo Pagliarini, a friend and constant supporter of the children, who died in June 1997, while this book was being translated; it is also dedicated to him.

And finally, thanks to all those who, voluntarily or involuntarily, who suggested to me that I am inexperienced in many of the discussed topics, ideas and proposals that, not being able to quote them, I have copied and used without any major scruples.

Acronyms[1]	
CNR	National Research Council
ISTAT	Italian National Institute of Statistics
ANCI	The National Association of Italian Municipalities
IAEC	International Association of Educating Cities

---

[1] Whenever possible, the acronyms have been translated to their corresponding English variant. If an English abbreviation does not exist for this institution, the original one has been used to facilitate further searches.

COOP	Italian consumers' cooperative
CGD	Democratic Parenting Coordinator
INU	Italian National Institute of Urban Planning
WWF	Wild World Foundation
MCE	Movement for Cooperative Education

Introduction

Citizens suffer the evils of the city, but they do not seem to ask, at least explicitly, for the city to change. They think that it is no longer possible, they have given up. They ask to live at least a little better, that their discomfort is reduced. They ask for more services to better withstand the discomfort of the city.

They know that those who suffer the most are the children, they don't know how to help them and so, more and more often, they decide not to have them or, simply stop having them: "How can you have children in these conditions?"

Those who have more awareness, more means, instead leave the city and go to live in small places or the countryside: "You only live once!"

Two ways of fleeing and of expressing helplessness and despair. Acts that leave the city more alone and defenseless.

But today in the city there is an important person, the mayor; important because his fellow citizens, and not his party, have given him the role of governing of the city. Probably, a mayor can win the votes to be re-elected by giving even better services, making the city more bearable, so that at the end of his term his constituents can say: "Today is better than four years ago" and decide to re-elect him. But if a mayor, rather than his re-election, thinks about the future of the city and the children and grandchildren of his fellow citizens, , he will set hope in motion. He must participate in a dream – believe that his city will be beautiful, healthy, safe again tomorrow; that he can have his children playing in the street once more. He must start working with his team, with all his adult colleagues, to see this dream become a reality, that being a child is worth it again.

In recent years, many Italian and foreign mayors, interpreting the needs of their fellow citizens and cities, have expressed interest in the project I present on these pages. In accepting the proposals, some of common sense, some bold, others provocative, I have noticed the urgency for a solution that the reasonable methods of politics and economics do not seem to be able to provide.

In response to this urgency, the book was born in a hurry. After many conferences, many meetings with the City commission government, many colloquiums, I thought an instrument was necessary to continue the debate on ideas and a comparison of initiatives. I apologize for the direct and informal form, the possible repetitions and the excessive underlining. It is a work material that wants to grow and improve thanks to the contribution of all those who want to recognize and use it.

First part:
The project

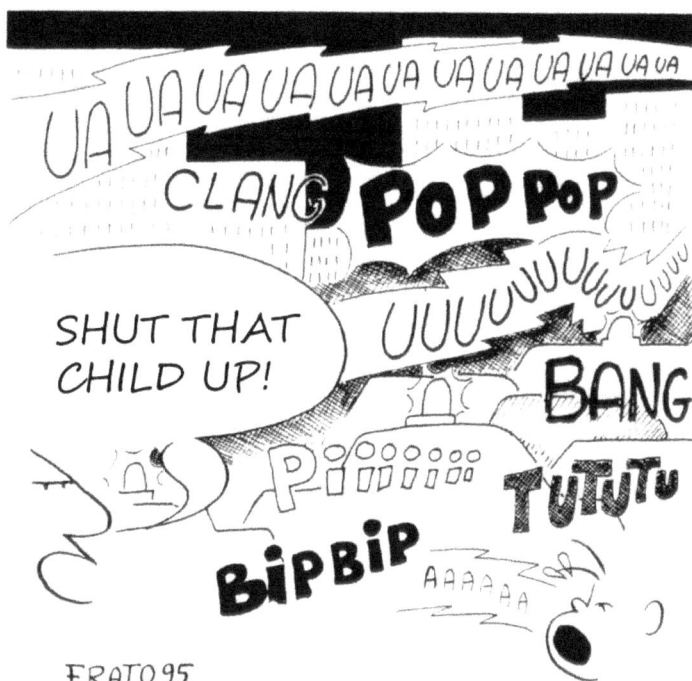

Chapter 1

Discomfort analysis

Background: before we were afraid of the forest

Before we were afraid of the forest. It was the forest of the wolf, the ogre, the darkness. It was the place where we could get lost. When our grandparents told us stories, the forest was the favorite place to hide traps, enemies, anguishes. As soon as the character entered the woods, we began to be afraid, we knew that something could happen, that something would happen. The story was slower, the voice more serious, we held each other and expected the worst. The forest was frightening with its shadows, its sinister buzzing, the gloomy song of the cuckoo, the branches that could suddenly catch you.

Instead, we felt safe among the houses, in the city, among the neighbors. This was the place where we looked for our pals and met up and played together. There, each one in his place, there we hid, there we organized the gang, to play visitors, to bury the treasure. It was the place where we built toys, according to the methods and skills taken from adults and taking advantage of the resources that the environment offered. It was our world.

Everything has changed over the course of a few decades. There has been a tremendous, rapid, and total transformation, as never seen before in our society, at least in any document of written history.

On the one hand, the city has lost its characteristics, it has become dangerous and hostile; on the other, the greens, environmentalists, animal protectors, have emerged, reclaiming the green and the forest. The forest has become beautiful, bright, the object of dreams and desire. The city has turned ugly, gray, aggressive, dangerous, monstrous.

The city

In the last decades, and resoundingly in the last fifty years, the city, born as a place of meeting and exchange, has discovered the commercial value of the space and has disrupted all the concepts of balance, well-being and coexistence, only developing plans in order to obtain benefits. It sold itself. Until very recently, the poor and the rich lived close to each other. Of course, their houses were different, some were of the poor and others of the rich, but they grew up in the same neighborhoods. Then, the land was given a different value according to its proximity to the city center and this upset everything.

The poor could not renovate their run-down shacks without assistance. They "preferred" to sell them to be able to move to the suburbs, all to exactly the same houses, identical to those shown on television.

Historic centers have become offices, banks, fast-food restaurants, headquarters of large companies, rich and sophisticated homes. At dusk, the city center empties and becomes dangerous, people are afraid to walk alone on the street, there are drug addicts, thieves, criminals. Historical centers, so different and rich derived from centuries of history and culture, from the pleasure of beautiful and not only useful things, are no longer the object of care and concern of their inhabitants. Children have been denied the experience of the most beautiful places in our country, their games, the walks and the memories of the elderly.

The suburbs, on the other hand, were born in a few years, without squares, without green, without monuments.

The suburbs are the same throughout the world – the same blocks, the same wide and straight streets, the same abandonment – because they were not born out of the long-term considerations of men wishing to have fitting and comfortable living spaces for themselves and their descendants, but rather out of an overwhelming impulse towards speculation.

The city no longer has inhabitants, it no longer has people who experience its streets, its spaces. The center is a place to work, to buy, to go to the office, but not to live. The suburbs are the place where you do not live, you only sleep... The city has lost its life.

The city has become the forest of our stories.

The medieval castle was large, powerful, rich and almost uninhabited, surrounded by hovels, by the slums of the township, where the peasants and craftsmen lived by means of their work and the protection offered by the lord of the castle.

When cities are born, this hierarchical link is broken and the citizens are in a common territory and, while maintaining diverse classes and conditions, share the space. The square becomes the symbol of the city and the Town Hall, the cathedral, the army headquarters and the market face this square. The city is the place where citizens meet to sell and buy, to defend themselves, to pray, to administer justice.

Today it seems that the city has returned to the medieval model – the rich and sparsely populated historical center, surrounded by a poor and sometimes miserable periphery, which depends on the rich center to survive.

The city has renounced being a place of meeting and exchange and has opted for *separation* and *specialization* as the new development criteria. A separation and specialization of spaces and competences – different places for different people, different places for different functions. The historic center for banks, luxurious stores, fun; the suburbs for sleep. There are also the places of the children – the nursery, the park, the library; the places of the elderly – day centers, retirement homes; the places of knowledge – from nursery school to university; specialized places for shopping – the supermarket, the mall. There is also the hospital, the place of the illness.

An example: family, home

Going to the hospital was once a completely exceptional event, as a result of serious illnesses and serious accidents. Disease was a domestic experience. Today people go to the hospital for any type of test, for a check-up, for examination: they are born, they suffer illness and die almost always away from home, in separate and specialized places. Families have lost the ability to endure such rich and strong experiences that put them to the test in pain and happiness, that demanded continuous adaptations and strengthened them. It is acknowledged that birth in a hospital has meant life for many women and for many children, but now, economic, hygienic and social conditions would allow the vast majority of families to have the extraordinary experience of childbirth in their own homes. This change, which is already taking place in many countries in northern Europe, would guarantee economic savings and give the possibility of being born within the family, between the arms of the father, close to siblings.[1] The same can be said for the majority of stages of diseases and the great experience of death. What then persists as a family experience? Only the routine, which is repeated without feeling or changes every day. There is much talk about family crisis; it would help to have important experiences like these to put the family back on its feet, to give it strength. This would require a clear will and availability to change, to move forward in a new way, keeping in mind the new conditions.

Together with the family, the home has also been transformed, responding to these new needs. It is a home without children, without elders. It has developed in height responding to the property speculation in urban areas and without thinking about how a four or five-year-old child can go and play with his friends, or how it can continue living without driving some old man crazy; who can no longer visit his regular places, walk, meet a friend. It is a home that no longer knows how to anticipate or withstand the uproar of children who play, while it has adapted very well to the awful noise of the

---

[1] Mumford (1945), who defines hospitals as "disease warehouses," referring to the American situation, already spoke of the need to avoid hospital birth (see Appendix 3).

sirens, of the horns. However, the stairs have always been a privileged place to play, as well as the hallways and playgrounds, and adults have always been able to accept and tolerate that healthy, though annoying, uproar of the playing children. For these small and old prisoners, they have invented the balconies, again separate, distant, fictitious spaces.

Another example: the mall

An environmentalist would say today that the city as a unitary environment, as an ecosystem, is disappearing and is becoming increasingly the sum of specialized, autonomous and self-sufficient places, each with its own parking lot, its own bar, ATM, security guard... In short, each place tends to be a small city. Before, buying meant taking a tour, entering different places, finding several people, each day the same, being able to resume the chat the next day by telling a secret, a story or communicating the latest news. Today, to buy, one moves to another area of the city, where you can buy everything, even only once a month. A typical example is that of the shopping center or mall, which is emerging on the edge of the city, proposing itself as a small, autonomous, efficient and enjoyable city. A city without cars, with streets and squares, safe for children, for whom specific and assisted spaces are often created. Where you can eat, do bank operations, go to the hairdresser and, naturally – buy, buy everything. A nice place for many families, where they meet and spend a Saturday together. The deterioration makes the city uninhabitable and we defend ourselves by building safe, protected places, where we can spend our free time in peace.

This is a constant trend in the city today, consistent with the logic of separation and specialization – creating services and increasingly independent and self-sufficient structures. This happens with the hospital, with the stadium, with the great museums, with the university campus.

The misunderstanding of services

The separation undoubtedly produces disgust, discomfort, creates confrontation between people with their own history, with their own affections, hinders the communication, the encounter, the solidarity. The city administrators, responsible for this perverse transformation of the characteristics of urban life, must somehow recover the consensus of their citizens and, above all, of their voters. If they did not do so, they would risk losing their power. In some cases, quite frequently, the administrators have preferred not to take care of the displease of the citizens and have won their consensus with dishonorable forms of electoral pacts; but these are not of interest to our discourse. On the other hand, in other cases, the administrators have taken charge of the displease of their fellow citizens and have developed, as compensation for the dislikes and as a guarantee of consensus, the policy of service. Public services have become the symbol and display of good administration: "Are you forced to live far from the urban center, away from the offices, the places of fun and culture? Do not worry. I put at your disposal even faster, more efficient means of public transportation". "Don't you know what to do with your children, don't you have the possibility or time to educate them? Do not worry. I will open nurseries, meeting centers, libraries…" "Don't you know how to take care of your elderly in your small apartment on the twelfth floor, with the work schedule you have? Do not worry, I offer you centers for the elderly, trips, vacations and retirement homes".[2]

Specialization qualifies the service and makes separation worthwhile. Children and elders are not allowed, or find it difficult, to live with their own family, in their own homes, in their city, but they receive the best care that modern psychology, pedagogy, paediatrics, dietetics, and geriatrics can offer. Even better than their family could. What is important is that the citizen who votes is satisfied for the short duration of the term. Politicians' time is short: they are assessed every four years; long-term projects do not yield instant results, and they do not secure votes.

In this whole affair, which may seem reasonable and even commendable, there's something disturbing, diabolical: the loss of hope, resignation. The city is given up on; services, the best services, assist in supporting it, with no hope of changing it: "It is the price of progress," "We cannot go back." It seems that progress is an "all-inclusive" global offer: the car and the washing machine, along with their advantages, inevitably lead to pollution, drugs, violence, fear. Altogether, either take it or leave it.

An Agreement between Adults

In this situation, which is difficult for everyone, the ones who suffer most are the children. With them, compensation—the economic assessment of damages—does not work. Services conceived for adults are not good for children. If we remove their small playing space at home and we return it a hundredfold, richer and bigger, one kilometer away, according to the laws of separation and of specialization we have in fact taken it away from them: they

---

[2] I met a man at the airport who was returning from a trip to Japan, where he had participated in a commercial exhibition. He had been housed in a hotel that was 150 kilometers from the place of the exhibition and every morning a train "shot" him in just half an hour from the hotel to his destination, the same time it takes me to travel the distance from home to the institute in Rome. An extremely efficient service that, however, makes it natural to have a person reside 150 kilometers from the city where he works!

can only go to the faraway park if they are taken by an adult, that is, they depend on the adult's schedule; they can only go if they change their clothes—otherwise it would be embarrassing to take them— but if they change their clothes they cannot get dirty, and if they cannot get dirty they cannot play; the person that goes with him has to wait for him, and while waiting they watch the child, and he cannot play under supervision.

The parks are an interesting example of how services are intended by adults for adults and not for children, even though these are the official recipients. These spaces for children are all the same (all over the world, or at least in the west), rigorously leveled, often fenced and always equipped with slides, swings and merry-go-rounds.

The first tool put to use during the development of a garden, a children's playground, is the steamroller. It seems that, according to adults, children like to play on flat ground when in reality the horizontal level prevents them from hiding, which is, by the way, an important part of the game. But the flat terrain does not require much vigilance. The child must play under supervision! We, adults, have quickly forgotten that play is linked to pleasure and pleasure is poorly associated with control and vigilance (let us think about our adult pleasure experiences!).

A second disturbing aspect is that it is the adults who indicate what games should be available for children in these places. The facilities are designed for repetitive, trivial activities, such as swaying, sliding and turning, as if the child is more like a hamster[3] than an explorer, an investigator, an inventor. They are the toys required for specific games, which should be used as adults have thought because, since children get bored very soon, in order to make them different and new, they try to use them in an unorthodox way and thus they also become dangerous: jumping off the moving carousel, sliding head-down the slide, swinging holding a single swing rope like a pirate when boarding a ship or holding the two ropes but upside down.

The playgrounds are all the same because they represent a stereotype – the presence of slides, swings and carousels ensures that the parent easily realizes that the administrator has used public money to build a service for their child. The fact that, in the end, children do not like it has very little importance.

Also, the other services for children are designed for adults and not for children. "We want childcare for working mothers," was said in the 1970s. In

---

[3] Turning on the wheel, which traditionally equips its cage, is not even liked by hamsters, who in their life in nature, in the Middle East, can undoubtedly experience more interesting and more risky adventures.

cities where there is plenty of employment for female workers, nurseries can remain open for up to ten or twelve hours a day, because this is the social demand of the workers. But what is the demand of the children? Undoubtedly, not to be left alone at home, but to have opportunities to meet their little friends. Can a child of one or two years old endure eight or ten hours in such a large place, exposed to forced socialization, to the uproar, to continuous stimuli, without the possibility of hiding, of escaping? We have not asked this. And instead, the adults, the nursery employees, are replaced to guarantee the service in three different shifts, because it is declared that they cannot support a workload greater than four or five hours a day!

Another every day and therefore disturbing example. When a conflict arises between the work schedules of adults and those of their children, for example, adults must clock in at eight and children must enter school at half-past eight, how do we react? Without any hesitation, in all cities, we ask the City Councils to create a new service, the "pre-school", that would welcome children from half-past seven – we end up making our children carry on their backs an hour more than we work. We could have thought of other solutions, we should have avoided that the little ones are the ones that are paying. We could have asked our unions to modify the work agreements so that if there is a child in a family who goes to school, one of the parents could make their work schedule flexible and enter after the classes start. I do not know if it would be possible to achieve this, but I am worried that we did not try and we did not even stop to think about it.

Chapter 2

So, what to do?

The city has become hostile to its own inhabitants, unsupportive and lacking in hospitality. The car is already the master of the city, it generates danger, noise and air pollution, vibrations, public-land occupation. The streets are dangerous, but we must live in this city and especially those who have children feel the need and the urgency to find a solution.

The private defense solution

The solution that our society vigorously spreads through the media, commercial production, its specialists (psychologists, educators, family consultants) is that of the individualist, the private one. It is the one that justifies the current situation as a necessary consequence and cost of progress and that makes recommendations such as: "Parents should be with their children more"; "There is no one better than mom and dad to be with the children"; "We must play more with our children". These suggestions naturally create an annoying contrast with the fast pace of life, with the hours of commuting, with the desire to relax a bit when you get home. They generate intense feelings of guilt. They put adults in the best conditions to take advantage of countless commercial products. Hence the double message that our society addresses to its citizens today – defend yourselves and buy.

First of all, then, the path of defense. The home understood as a fallout shelter: outside – danger, the wicked, traffic, drugs, violence, the dark and menacing forest; inside – security, autonomy, tranquility, the safe little house of the three little pigs or, if you prefer, the fortified medieval castle with the raised bridge. Armored doors with peepholes are placed to see without being seen; intercoms with video, alarm systems are installed. The rules of the neighborhood association prevent strangers from entering. The child is taught not to open the door to anyone, not to stop to talk to anyone, to accept nothing from strangers.[1]

---

[1] And then in school, but also in democratic families, it is intended to educate children about tolerance, solidarity, peace, and multiculturalism, which would be equivalent to being open to others, believing in others and be convinced that others have something important to give us!

And, finally, buy more, because luckily, commercial production is sensitive to the needs of modern people. Everything that contributes to us feeling good and calm, alone, even for a long time, is inside the home: television, video, videogames and toys, toys until you say 'enough is enough'.

In our houses, a strange sensation is perceived, a kind of pride for having made them able to resist an unknown danger that could arise. The interior is neat, comfortable, relaxing, while the exterior is chaotic, overwhelming and upsetting. The freezer is full of food that can last for months, the video collection allows us to have the movies that we like the most in our house. In our houses, we will be well whatever happens outside! It is the exasperated private confinement.

Before, almost everything was invested in the city, in the public. The house was modest, it served for the bare minimum. The real "room" was the city, which must be beautiful, cozy, suitable for walking, for a meeting, for spending, for playing. Today, the trend has been reversed, everything is invested privately, in the home, which becomes increasingly like a refuge and a fortress.

Defending yourself, solving each problem on your own, locking yourself up at home means leaving the city. The abandoned city becomes even more dangerous, aggressive, inhuman. So, we must strengthen the defensive means and behavior. But these will produce greater isolation and abandonment and, in turn, will determine an increase in environmental danger. Thus, a perverse spiral develops, with no future.

We already have several signs for this process, in our society and in other, more "developed" societies. In recent years, in our cities, there has been a rapid and progressive militarization: local police have been armed; more and more private security guards have appeared alongside banks, public and private entities. Personal controls, metal detectors, have also increased when entering the airport, the bank, with electronic controls also at the exit of some stores, bookstores, supermarkets. There are armored windows that protect the ticket offices of the stations and to ask for a ticket we must speak through amplifiers, exactly like in the booths of the maximum-security prisons. We have reached the absurd – they use sirens to transport postal values, continuous fears and distress, because of money! And we are no longer surprised by all of this, they seem like adequate and legitimate defenses.

In the United States, after having armed the doors, ordinary citizens have armed themselves and in one of their states, students are allowed to go to school with weapons. Fortunately, this news seems abhorrent to us,[2] they still

---

[2] Today, in the United States, there are eight million people who work in security companies, many more than those who work in metallurgy!

horrify us, but they are only the coherent consequence of the perverse spiral of defense and violence.

The social solution of participation

There is a second way, a second solution, contrary to defense. It is the one that rejects the resignation and condemns this hasty "progress", desired only by some, in the service of interests that have nothing to do with the public good, with the happiness of the citizens, with the quality of life. It is the one that considers that the problem is not individual and personal, but social and political. It is the solution that aims for the trend to change, for the city to change; that does not want to go back, but that wants to move forward in a different, new way, appropriate to the complexity and richness of today's world, but without renouncing the social, the solidarity, the happiness.

The average citizen

Until now, and with greater emphasis in the recent decades, the city has been thought, planned and evaluated, taking as a parameter an average citizen with the characteristics of an adult, man and worker, and that corresponds to the strong voter. In this way, the city has lost the non-adult citizens, non-men and non-workers, second-class citizens, with fewer rights or without them.

To get on the bus or train, you have to be in good physical condition, well trained, because to get on you have to conquer a slope of almost half a meter. A child, an older person or even just a woman with a narrow skirt would not be successful in the endeavor.

The new, crowded and ugly neighborhoods of the suburbs are called "bedroom communities." But, a "bedroom" for whom? Only for the working adults who leave in the morning and return at night. Their children, their parents, often even their wives, live there. For them, those neighborhoods are not a "bedroom", but a "residence". And then it makes no sense to characterize them with that name as if we justified the absence of social, meeting and leisure places, because "after all, you only sleep there".

The child as a parameter

The proposal is, therefore, to replace the average citizen, adult, man and worker with the *child*.

It is not about offering initiatives, opportunities, new structures for the children, or defending the rights of a weak social component. It is not about modifying, updating, or improving the services for children, which obviously remains an important duty of the public administration.

Instead, it is about getting the administration to lower its eyes to the height of the child, in order to not lose sight of any of them.

It is about accepting the intrinsic diversity of the child as a guarantee of all diversities.

The objection of those who claim that the children are not the only inhabitants is irrelevant, because it is about adopting a new perspective, a new philosophy to evaluate, program, plan and modify the city. Anyone capable of contemplating the needs and desires of children will have no difficulty in taking into account the needs of the elderly, of the disabled, of people from other communities. Because the fundamental problem is learning to accept diversity, and the child is diverse, the child probably differs even more from his father than a white adult differs from a black adult.

It is assumed that when the city is more suitable for children, it will be more suitable for all.

It is a concrete proposal, born from an experience initiated in 1991 by the Italian City Council of Fano[3] and that today raises the interest and unity of many Italian and foreign cities.

It is a proposal with the mayor as a natural role model, who guarantees and positions it at the base of the proposals of his administration policy of the city.[4] It is an option that the local government shares, considering it a continuous test and an indirect effort that "pollutes" the activity of all the departments and all administrative actions, from urban to sanitary, from leisure to commercial.

---

[3] Fano is a city of about 60,000 inhabitants, on the Adriatic coast, in the Marche region, between Pesaro, Urbino and Ancona. It is of Roman origin (*Fanum Fortunae*), rich in Romanesque and Baroque monuments. Its traditional economy was divided between port activity and agriculture. Currently, its inhabitants make a living from fishing, spa tourism and small industries.

[4] The new Italian electoral law, which allows citizens to directly elect the mayor quite autonomously with respect to the parties and gives the municipal agent the power to appoint his own government team, with his own program and the possibility of exhausting the legislature, makes him the true democratic representative of the city. In these first years of experience and at such a difficult time for Italian politics, it seems that the mayors are precisely the people who are proposing a new way of doing politics in Italy.

Chapter 3

Why the child precisely?

Why take on the child as a parameter of change? The election is not intended to be provocative or paradoxical. It has precise psychological and sociological motivations, important historical background, high moral significance and also, I believe, strong political weight.

Childhood in the history of mankind: the supremacy of the game

It is not true that the child does not know anything, that it is a blank sheet on which everything should be written and that the responsibility and merit of the first and fundamental teachings will correspond to the school. The truth is the opposite. The child's development is faster precisely in the first days, in the first months and in the first years of life, according to the results of scientific research. The explosion occurs after birth and not around the age of six with the start of the so-called age of reason. Before a child enters a school classroom for the first time, the most decisive things have already happened – the most important learnings, those on which all subsequent knowledge must be built, have already been acquired or, otherwise, can hardly be recovered.

But how can such a disconcerting phenomenon be explained? In the first years of life, there are no teachers, no teaching materials are used, nor are programs written. So, to what can we attribute the merit of such important progress? It seems to me that we have no alternative but to attribute it to the most significant activity of these first years – playing. Why does this children's activity have such great power? While playing, the child has an experience uncommon in the life of the adult – that of dealing with the complexity of the world alone. The child with its permanent curiosity, with everything it knows and knows how to do, with everything it does not know and wants to know, in front of the world with all its stimuli, its novelties, its fascination. And playing means cutting out a detail of this world every time – a detail that will include a friend, objects, rules, a space to occupy, time to manage, chances to take. With total freedom, because what cannot be done is invented. It is precisely thanks to this complexity that in the first years the most important lessons of the human life are carried out. No adult can anticipate or measure how much a playing child learns and that amount will always be higher than we could imagine. No one can schedule or accelerate this process, at the risk of preventing or worsening it. Perhaps it would be more useful for children if this knowledge was kept hidden since if it were to reach the ears of adults, they could think of helping them, supporting them with appropriate teaching and educational materials. The main condition of this marvel would end up missing, that is to say that adults "let children do", "let children play". The child's game, before and outside of school, is "wasting time," is being lost in time, consists of encountering the world in an exciting relationship, full of mystery, risk, adventure. And the driving force is one of the most powerful known to man – pleasure. That is why a child, when playing, can even forget to eat. The child's free and spontaneous play resembles the highest and most extraordinary experiences of the adult, such as scientific research, exploration, art, mysticism. Precisely, the experiences in which the adult finds himself facing complexity, in which he finds again the possibility of letting himself be driven by the great force of pleasure.

Educational proposals, although necessary, move instead on a lower level, less stimulating and therefore less productive.[1] In the educational proposal, the student ends up deprived of the exciting encounter with the complexity and the chill of cutting a part of the world autonomously. It is the adult who proposes a portion of that complex world to the student, so that the required activity produces the desired learning with certainty and in the expected time. Thus, detached from the whole, that fragment of the world loses all its fascination and mystery, becomes incomprehensible, and serves only to be learned in school. To be more certain of the result, teachers tend to replace the complexity of the real world with that of the more controllable educational proposal, the exercise, the textbook. The control is thus absolute, but in general, the result is poor, almost always inferior to the expectations and contradictory – while learning, the student rejects what they teach them, does not make it its own, does not change thanks to it. A parallel learning is born, which serves only in school, until the last class subject, until the last exam and then it's over. In school, for example, we all know that it is the sun that is still with respect to Earth which orbits it. But in everyday life, we all continue to say, and we will probably continue to think, that the sun rises and sets, that is to say, it moves. This is said every day, even on television!

School, with this simplification, with the certainty of its programs, has completely lost the connection with pleasure and must resort to a much less powerful and effective driving force, that of duty.

---

[1] "What teachers we were, when we had no concern with teaching!" (Homel translation), writes Pennac (1992), referring to the fascinating experience of reading with the child in the first years in the face of the explosion of the reading proposed by the school.

The cities have forgotten about the children

The editorial of the first issue of the Italian magazine *Urbanística* of 1945, written by Lewis Mumford[2], observes how the city has forgotten its citizens, starting with the children. And Mumford begins this essay by citing the writings of Joseph K. Hart who, in 1925, held the same ideas. The thesis of the two authors, long before the urban disaster in the western world, with the great building speculation of the sixties and seventies, is based on the consideration that cities, in their recent development, have forgotten the greatest part of the citizens, specifically the children, but also the women, the young people and the elderly. They have been designed only for the strongest category of citizens – the adult and production. Hence, the proposal to rethink the city reflecting on the demands of the different ages of life. Some of the solutions pointed out by Mumford are naive or, at times, unconvincing, but it is interesting that more than five decades ago, such a clear awareness of the mistakes that were made and the advanced and multidisciplinary planning sensitivity was already present in the world of architecture and urban planning. In his article, Mumford makes a timely critique of the separation between generations and between the functions that the modern city has caused. He criticizes the widespread use of hospitals and advises the return of childbirth at home or in small neighborhood clinic houses. It points out the need to create places where children can play, unconventional and non-stereotypical but rich in the variety of elements and hiding places. It proposes the commitment of adolescents, in the form of community service for the maintenance of common spaces, in response to the foreseeable economic difficulties of local administrations for the care of gardens and parks. He denounces the danger of the tendency to isolate the big city and claims, instead, the right to loneliness and recollection. It suggests the social use of schools in extracurricular hours. Recommends the inclusion of the elderly in social life, avoiding the separation and triumph of the institutions. Urban planning, in short, must guarantee the return to the human ladder – "a constantly variable combination of a multitude of associative activities, variable in intensity and duration and in continuous development, through the cycle of life, from birth to death". All this in 1945!

It is also significant that the magazine *Urbanística*, in its first issue of 1945, just after the war, has chosen to publish this writing. To get out of the misery, the ruins, the moral and material destruction of our country, it spoke about children and not about economic options or speculation in urban areas. This

[2] See the article "The planning for the different stages of life", by Lewis Munford, reproduced in Appendix 3.

makes the liability of those who, in the following decades, not only have not taken the children into account but have insisted on denying the rights of the weakest citizens only for their eagerness to obtain their own personal benefit in a prejudiced and guilty way even more serious.

The child is alone

This century, along with many other merits and within the boundaries of the rich West, can be considered, fairly, as the child's century. Never before have the fundamental rights of the child been recognized and defended as they are today. Medical advancements have almost nullified the risk of death and serious trauma in newborns – the few children born have a high probability of getting older.

In the recent past, many children did not survive birth, many suffered irreversible traumas due to inappropriate obstetric and newborn care practices. Those of the less wealthy social classes, that is, the vast majority of the population, grew up in large families and in total promiscuity. Not everyone started elementary school and almost everyone dropped out after a few years, with several suspensions and largely illiterate. For most of them, work experience began before the age of ten, as apprentices, as assistants. Heavy work, a long schedule that left little time for children's games, often without pay, in exchange for learning. The parents' relationship with the child, especially the father and the employer, was hard, often violent. A condition, therefore, difficult and, of course, not privileged.

Today, the child's right to childhood, to play, to go to school, to not be exploited for work is firmly defended. His father cannot violate these rights either, under penalty of losing parental rights. The child cannot be offended, cannot be beaten, cannot be discriminated against. Even the different child, from another culture, from another religion or disabled, enjoys the rights of all, goes to a mainstream school, must be properly integrated. All this was unthinkable no more than half a century ago.

For several decades, psychological research has been almost obsessively dealing with the child's world, its drives, its thinking, its logic, its language. Their first sentences are collected, their spontaneous knowledge is studied, their scribbles are analyzed. Researchers look for the roots, the explanation of the human in the child.

Books that collect thoughts, writings, children's drawings are published. Films that illustrate the life of the child are shot, television programs are broadcast that have children as their only protagonists, with their often-unpredictable answers to the difficult questions posed by adults.

National and international congresses are dedicated to children – in 1989 the United Nations approved the Convention on the Rights of the Child and Unesco dedicated that same year to the child.

But precisely in this historical period, the child is affected by a new affliction, unknown to his little predecessors – loneliness.

We can consider this loneliness as a consequence of the vertiginous progress and the growing well-being or, if you prefer, as a social cost that taxes the comforts of our lives of rich Westerners.

The child is alone because more and more often it is an only child

Being an only child not only deprives the child of the company of his peers within the family, but also deprives him of intermediate models between himself and adults, models that make the comparisons less distressing and the learning easier. Being an only child means facing all the expectations of two adults alone, without mitigating, without help. It means being subject to excessive dedication by parents, who will find it increasingly difficult to recognize in their child's own autonomy their need and right to leave, to gradually separate from them.

A prisoner in their fortress home

The lack of company at home has become more serious due to the impossibility of going to look for it outside – outside are the dangers that drive adults, not without reason, to protect the child by preventing them from leaving. Then, the attitude of defense, that was spoken of before, is adopted. The house is "armed" and the child is locked in it, instilling suspicion and distrust before everything and before everyone. What does it mean to be born and to grow up in a fortress home in the midst of distrust of others, and in the midst of the terror about what surrounds us?

Entrusted to a modern and efficient babysitter: the television

This modern and increasingly perfect appliance is a corollary of the child's loneliness. It is one of the parents' best collaborators that will begin to create some problems later when the child goes to school, as it threatens to steal time from homework, from "work", but in the first years, it is a great help. An authentic, economical and efficient babysitter. But what happens in this intimate relationship that the child has with television, oblivious to parental control?

It is difficult to know exactly what cognitive, affective, social and physical mechanisms the constant and prolonged viewing of television programs produces in children. On the one hand, it produces, without a doubt, knowledge. Television is capable of offering increasingly better, rich in information and attractive services, programs and documentaries. Without a doubt, today our children learn more through television than through school. However, these notions and knowledge are always seen and heard. The hands serve less and less; the child does not learn to do; so, he is alone, in his immobility.

Together with the highest-quality broadcasts, the child absorbs, however, many low-content programs, cartoons that are violent, poorly made, unscrupulous as mere commercial products, mass-produced, underusing computerized systems. And finally, it watches all the programs where the violence of the show and the rawness of the information are thought up by adults. There are almost always programs that the child sees alone, without the possibility of dialogue, of shared distraction – the child alone with the television. Fears get inside that cannot be exorcised and end up showing up in the middle of the night, with a bad dream, a nightmare...

In this intimate and intense dialogue (carry out the experiment to observe the absorbed gaze of a child in front of the television) there is a very disturbing manipulation of our children, of which even the state-television entity becomes complicit – in the spaces dedicated to children, broadcast advertisements are addressed directly to them so that they become persuaders of consumption before their parents. The manipulation is serious because it raises useless needs within the child, which will negatively modify its personality, in the continuous search for new things, progressively losing the ability to appreciate and utilize them well, and entering the perverse logic of using and throwing. It is also serious because the child becomes a powerful claimant before the parents, in whom the feeling of guilt can be mobilized for being so little present in the child's life. Parents buy without realizing the origin of this request, which is often interpreted as a spontaneous idea of the child, to which, therefore, cannot be denied.

The child as a minor

The child today experiences a very delicate and disturbing situation. As the child is, increasingly, a scarce asset within the family, they tend to overvalue it, pamper it and protect it and, consequently, to separate and marginalize it more and more from the world of adults. The child is commonly called "minor", and this is defined in the laws, in the speeches of experts and politicians, in the programs of political parties. We are all younger or older than someone, depending on the point of view or the parameter taken into account, but the child is always "minor" by definition. This means that a fundamental right, the right to the present, to today is not recognized. The child is worth what it will be, what it will become, not what it is, it is only entitled to the future. It is a future citizen, not a citizen. The school career is a precise confirmation of this attitude – each school level is preparatory for the next, each teacher is concerned that the students are prepared for the demands of the level that follows, that they are appreciated by the classmates that will come. The school prepares for tomorrow, prepares for school, despite the laws, despite the theories. It does not prepare, however, for today, for life. It does not value the past.

If the child is a minor, then it is always in danger and is therefore protected and defended. A dangerous policy of helping children is being developed, of child-support telephones. A policy that is based on the emphasis of the police report, on danger, on the probability of violence. Increasingly alarming data, often not elaborated or used correctly, end up confirmed and emphasized by not many, but resounding cases of which newspapers and television speak. This probability justifies the fear, the continuous vigilance, the segregation of children by their parents. It reduces autonomy, prevents the development of self-defenses.

Children are not protected, but "armed," that is, equipped with resources, ability, autonomy.

With this, we do not want to propose that the means of defense be renounced in the face of macro violence that, unfortunately, exists, but to make them effective – decentralized in the Town Halls and therefore capable of immediate intervention. We want to propose that these means not be sustained with alarming advertising, because the safety of our children will depend on the trust that adults know how to give to their children and not on fear and defense. Violence with minors is almost always the result of the same logic of closure, segregation, defense. It happens in private, inside the home, in places of security. And if it happens outside the home, it takes advantage of the abandonment, the disinterest. Let's try to talk less about violence, favor more well-being, participation, the possibility of sharing, and violence will decrease.

Let us all commit ourselves not to use the horrible adjective "minor" again, and to call children "children."

The child is stronger

It is worth betting on the child because the child is paradoxically stronger. The proposal that is being illustrated in this book is very close to the environmental proposal – we want to promote a reversal of the trend in political choices and individual attitudes to make our cities more habitable; to guarantee a better world and sustainable development to those who come after us. The problem of the environmental proposal is its difficulty of being understood. There are not many who can understand what *ecology* means and recognize its multidisciplinary and interdisciplinary weight, and complexity. If the concept of *ecology* is trivialized by reducing it to plants and animals, or is associated only with pollution and waste, then it becomes unbelievable or of little effect. People, unfortunately, do not give up their comfortable habits and do not modify already consolidated behaviors to save the plants or keep the city clean.

I think it is more powerful to propose, instead, that we modify our attitudes and our habits for something concrete, understandable, close and important like our children and our grandchildren. I don't know if it will be enough, but I think it's the best card that we have to play. The child is our past; a past that is often forgotten too soon, but that will help us live better with our children and make fewer mistakes if we keep it alive within us. The child is our present, because most of our efforts and our sacrifices are destined for it. The child is our future, the society of tomorrow, which can continue or betray our choices and our expectations. For these reasons, the child is strong, even though fewer children are born today, although it seems that adults fear them, or maybe even for that reason.

The position of the elder is different and if the elders are more, we have greater difficulties in identifying with them. No one has already been old and probably nobody wants to become old. For this reason, perhaps the initiatives that are born in favor of the elderly, although with the best intentions, end up being merely assistive and isolating.

The child is stronger for one last and important reason – it is not easily corruptible. And this is not because children cannot be easily manipulated – we parents know that we have used toys, rewards and punishments for a long time to "convince" children to do what we think is right. The publicity aimed at children to force us, adults, to buy it is well known. The child is not corruptible with respect to the options of the city because it has not participated in its deterioration, because the solutions adopted so far to adapt to the discomfort described at the beginning have never taken into account its demands. They have always been, as we have seen, solutions of agreement between adults and for adults, and therefore it, the child, has not benefited from them. If we choose, then, the child as a new parameter of change, we must choose a completely new path for which the old balances, the old commitments will no longer have value.

"Unless you become like little children…"

Finally, we cannot forget the phrase pronounced two thousand years ago by Jesus of Nazareth, which remains one of the most mysterious, most puzzling and most fascinating expressions of the Gospel: "Unless you change and

become like little children, you will never enter the kingdom of heaven."
(Matthew 18, 3).

Jesus says that you have to become - not be again - like children. In this case,
therefore, it is not an invitation to go back, but a revolutionary project to move
forward. You have to become like children to be worthy of the kingdom of
heaven. It is necessary to become small, therefore, to obtain the supreme, the
promise, the aim of the coming of Christ. This invitation to adopt the small ones
as a parameter is further reinforced when the poor are pointed out as a model:
"Blessed are the poor ...". Two categories without power, without value, in the
Hebrew society, become a parameter of salvation. Not only in the eschatological
sense, that is to say, referring to a future life, but also a parameter of holiness
and therefore of the right choice today, the historical path to happiness. Being
children and being poor means knowing how to be content, knowing how to
desire, to be free – necessary conditions for human happiness.

But something is changing

Until a few years ago, when there was full confidence in the economic and
consumer solutions, in the norms of the specialists and particularly in those
of technology, such a statement, that things can and must be started again
from the children, would have caused sympathetic smiles and the description
of those who supported the affirmation as dreamers or madmen. Today,
radical proposals like this one attract the attention of many citizens, many
mayors, and all children. We are starting to tire of the city's power, we are
beginning to no longer believe in "reasonable" solutions. We are beginning to
no longer be able to take it.

It should also be noted that, even in an incoherent and inconsistent manner,
there are already signs of rejection, on the one hand, of society's development
principles, such as the separation and specialization, and, on the other, signs
of recognition of the need for challenges at higher levels, that almost always
find children as witnesses and reference points.

For years, the productive forces denounce an overly sectoral, specialized,
and therefore rigid school education in the face of frequent changes in
technologies and productive processes, which require more creative, more
open, more adaptable training.

Also, in the form of industrial production (the production that, somehow,
invented the most exacerbated specialization down to the assembly line)
signs of critical review are appearing. A large Italian motorcycle factory is
experimenting with entrusting the complete assembly process of a moped to
a single worker. A worker who, therefore, will feel like the creator of the

product, the artisan somehow, with a great advantage of increased motivation and satisfaction.

Proceeding to the new things that directly concern the children, we must remember that a framework legislation for a National Action Plan for Children has been presented in the Italian Parliament that envisages the formation of a parliamentary commission and a national observatory; and that the Ministry of the Environment has assumed responsibility for a program with the title *The sustainable city custom-made for the boys and girls.*

Finally, the Italian Association of Juvenile Court, in 1996, sent a letter to the mayors asking them for "a city government that, not only in words, is tailored to the needs of girls and boys."

Second part:
The proposals

Chapter 4

A laboratory: "The city of children"

For the realization of this project, of this new philosophy of city governing, different paths can be followed. It may be the mayor who directly reveals the spirit of his program; however, it may be the citizens, through movements or associations, who propose and sustain it from the base. Here, the first way is described and somehow favored, followed in Fano since 1991[1], and that stands today in the different cities that are joining this project – the one that sees the mayor as an outstanding reference and that anticipates the opening of a laboratory dedicated to the elaboration and development of the project "The city of children". The City Council that opens a similar service, which dedicates staff and resources, in fact opens in its interior a sharp but exciting contradiction.

The Laboratory must assume the priority function of the "talking cricket" of Pinocchio, the conscience of the mayor and the government commission, protesting every time the agreed commitment is not fulfilled; and if this happened frequently, the presence of the Laboratory would become uncomfortable. Opening the Laboratory means, therefore, accepting a permanent conflict because the contrast between the child and the adult will never end, it will always move a little further into the future.

This conflict is, however, exciting, a stimulus of great wealth and of a high-level political debate, for being real, concrete, far from the political television jargon. It is about considering the city as a laboratory, a place of investigation, where you are willing to profoundly modify the outlook, perspectives, objectives.

The Laboratory will have an "educational" function with respect to administrators and citizens – it must put, or replace, the child in their head, that is, it must help adults to recognize children, their needs, their rights; to listen to them and to understand them. Not a simple endeavor, which requires preparation and great intellectual freedom.

The Laboratory will have a municipal administration cost, but a relative one. It should have a moderate budget that allows it to act, as far as possible,

---

[1] See the file n.1: "Fano: 'The city of children'".

without resorting to subsidies, with some autonomy and independence, with staff and in municipal premises; that guarantees their activities with children; makes the different initiatives known; is able to have some consulting if necessary. On the other hand, for the plans of changing the city, the Laboratory will not need its own resources, but it will have to "infect" the different councils so that the funds of the regular budget are spent in a different way; not for new things, but to carry out those already planned, with a new point of view. Therefore, it is not about spending more, but spending better. The Laboratory's function is not to become a structure that acts autonomously, but to develop a new philosophy of city governing within the administration and with the administration.

The danger of this proposal is that it is accepted with great enthusiasm, but it could also be relegated and trivialized with the same enthusiasm. A disturbing sign in this regard is the frequent unanimous vote with which the municipal plenary sessions approve projects that concern these initiatives related to children. If everyone agrees, it can be assumed that they believe it is not a risky option that aims to produce radical changes; that they do not realize that everything we will have to give back to the children (to the elderly, to the disabled) we must take away from those who until now have had it as a privilege; who do not think that voting to join the "City of Children" project means slowing traffic, returning space to pedestrians, bicycles, returning places to people. And then, the great fear is that in the face of a proposal in favor of children, it is not possible to say no, but in the end, in giving this satisfaction to the little ones, the serious discourse of the economy, the market, the competition and the elders is resumed from where it was left.

Give the floor to children

The first and most important action to be undertaken is to give children the role of protagonists, give them the floor, allow them to express opinions; and that adults are willing to listen to them, of wishing to understand them and have the will to take into account what they say. Naturally, what is proposed for children is valid for all citizens, for the elderly, for the disabled, for those of other communities. Again, the child opens the way and serves as a guarantee for everyone.

No one can represent the children without caring about consulting them, involving them, listening to them. Making children talk does not mean asking them to solve the problems of the city created by us. Instead, it means learning to take their ideas and proposals into account. It is not easy to give the floor to children or understand what they say. Gianni Rodari spoke of the "green" ear (in the sense of immature) that adults should have in order to know how to listen to children.[2] It takes a lot of curiosity, attention, sensitivity, simplicity. It is necessary to be convinced that children have things to tell us and give us, and they are different from what we know, and are capable of doing as adults do and that, therefore, it is worth letting them express what they really think. To do this, we must help children free themselves from stereotypes, the obvious and trivial answers that both television and the bad example of adults have put before their eyes at home, at school, in the city, hiding their desires, their creativity. Children must be encouraged to dare, to want, to invent, and then their ideas, their proposals, their contributions will emerge. Finally, we must know how to understand children, going beyond the apparent simplicity of their proposals. Then, these ideas will allow us not only to take into account the demands of the children, but to make the city better for all.[3]

To make this possible, the Laboratory must train new professionals capable of inspiring groups of children and young people with the different forms of democratic participation in the life of the city. As an example, we cite below two experiences that will be documented in the files of the third part of this book.

The Children's Council

The Laboratory asks a group of children to collaborate, to guarantee the child's point of view. It is not about offering children the game of imitating the

---

[2] One day as I took the train direct to Capranica-Viterbo/ a man got on with an ear as green as an unripe tomato./ He wasn't exactly young at all, but rather somewhat older./ Except for his bright green ear, he was totally, totally in order./ I quickly moved and changed my seat/ to study this phenomenon from head to feet./ "Sir," I said to him, "I see you've reached a certain age,/ so why a green ear at this late stage?"/ "Just say," he answered with courtesy, "that I've become quite old./ This ear is now the only thing left from my youth—if truth be told./ This ear, a child's ear, is used to help me grasp what I can—/ those voices adults don't ever hear and will never understand./ I listen to what the birds say, to the words of all the trees./ I listen to the clouds that pass as well as the rocks and streams./ I understand the children when they say some things I hear,/ those things that seem so strange to every grown-up's ear."/ That's what he said there with an ear as green as an unripe tomato/ on the day that I took the train direct to Capranica-Viterbo. (Translation by Jack Zipes)

[3] In Geneva, in the 1980s, a program for restructuring playgrounds for children was carried out, trying to avoid the topical solutions and meet the authentic playful demands of the children. It was observed that these spaces also met the demands of the adult citizens and especially the elderly, who enjoyed them greatly (Guichard, Ader, 1991).

behavior of adults in a miniature City council,[4] or a serious proposal of civic education, which are, in any case, noble objectives, but rather of giving the city the unprecedented opportunity to be confronted with a point of view and with "another" thought, different, like the child's. A Children's Council, therefore, to change the city and not to make children happy. The entertainers of the Laboratory must, on the one hand, ensure that children express themselves freely and authentically and, on the other, find the appropriate ways to give force to children's thoughts, so that the mayor and his councilors have to listen to them and bear them in mind more and more.[5]

The project-executing children

A second way of participating in the life of the city is the contribution that children can make in projects by offering their ideas and their proposals for the solution of the different urban problems that are presented. Some time ago, the president of the College of Architects of an Italian province questioned the Fano Laboratory's decision to entrust the children with the role of the architects, considering it inappropriate. The controversy was not trivial and rude, but intended to deepen a novelty that surprises and even perplexes the specialist who is institutionally responsible for the projects. This conflict was also a reason for reflection and clarification for us.

Inviting children to design real spaces and structures of the city, in collaboration with specialists such as urban planners, architects, psychologists, etc., does not mean delegating the task of carrying out a project that will always be linked to an enabling title to the children. An adult will be the organizer and responsible for the work done (we will not be able to report a child for not having planned the drainage in the plan of a small garden). It means, in fact, also opening the possibility of contributing and participating to children.

Today, the experience of "participatory architecture" is frequent, that is, of the participation of the users in defining the characteristics of the work requested by the specialist. The architect in charge of carrying out a new urban center can receive from the City Council, its contractor, the indication

---

[4] The imitation of adult behaviors has always been one of the fundamental bases of children's play (from war to the doctor, from mom and dad to the shop keeper) and I am sure, therefore, that those children having the experience of the Children's City Council have a wonderful experience. I doubt, however, that they have a direct and intense impact on the life of the city and on the activity of adult administrators. This was and is, on the other hand, the only objective of the project we are talking about and for this, until now, this form of participation of children in the city's choices has been preferred.

[5] See file n.2: "The Children's council".

to consult the recipients of his work, the neighborhood committee, the associations of the area, to know their requirements and their possible ideas and proposals. These consultations are carried out with meetings, debates, and surveys. But if we wanted to extend this form of participation to children, how could we do it? How does one get to know the needs and ideas of children? Not with surveys and debates, no doubt, but, for example, through drawing and practical activities. Designing is a good technique to know what children think.

Through design, by freeing themselves from stereotypes, freeing the creativity, children compare reality, their needs, their desires and possible solutions. Devising a project, even the making of a model, requires from children, in addition to the important phases of discussion and graphic design, specific operations such as manipulating, coloring, pasting, of which all children are capable. This means that the experience does not consider selecting "smart" children in verbal, written and graphic expressions, as is usually the case in school activities, and thus makes it an especially significant proposal. Even the most imaginative project can help an attentive and interested adult to learn about children's thinking and, through it, to find new, more beautiful and fairer solutions.

To achieve this, we must train new professionals capable of working with children. They may be architects, urban planners, psychologists, pedagogues, naturalists, sociologists or any others who, renouncing their own specific knowledge, are willing to do new things: help children observe within themselves dissatisfactions and desires, allow them to free themselves from stereotypes, awaken in them a new desire to dare more, to ask for more, to release the creativity and fantasy in a dialogue, always possible, but never dismissive of reality, of costs, of laws.

Finally, we will know the needs and wishes of the children, which probably cannot be translated into practice as expressed by them, but may be precious indications for the person in charge of carrying out the project. We can be sure that if the children get to participate in the city's projects, they will feel it, today as children and tomorrow as adults, as "theirs", a city to be taken care of and defended, as we all do with our home.[6]

Allowing children the experience of participating in a project does not only mean benefiting from their ideas and their contribution; it also means committing to new options, to profound changes in the habits of an administration. I refer, for example, to the times of bureaucracy, which are

---

[6] See file n.4: "The project-executing children".

traditionally often considered necessary and objective, but which in general are the result of the inertia and poor organization of services. If the children's project is approved it should mean that they can see it realized while they are still children; not after three or four years, but after a few months. If there are difficulties, it is necessary to inform the children, help them understand and continue the process. In childhood years, time counts a lot, it changes rapidly, expectations, needs, tastes change. If too much time passes, children lose interest and affirm themselves in the conviction that the elders are always the same, willing and quick to promise but slow to deliver.

This should be avoided because, otherwise, we would obtain the opposite result. Then it is better not to make any commitments – if it is considered that nothing can change in practice, in habits, in times, we should recognize with sincerity that the city cannot become the children's city.

I think it is clear that everything that has been said for children is equally valid for all citizens. Citizens lose their sense of the city, of projects, of promises, in the complicated bureaucratic itinerary, in the continuous delegation of responsibilities, in the incomprehensible extension of deadlines.

The child in the adults' mind

In order for the child to become a true protagonist, it is important to help adults develop a new sensitivity: the mayor, the municipal government commission, the leaders and specialists of the City Council must receive help to consider the reality of the children, their requirements and the gaps in the city with respect to the demands. It is worth working with the local police, with the elderly, with the doctors of the pediatric hospital, with the vendors, with all those professionals and social sectors that may have a relevant role in helping children regain their autonomy. It is important to work with teachers so that the school becomes a school increasingly suitable for children, that they can recognize and love, of which they can be proud. All efforts should naturally aim to change the attitude of all adults, and especially parents, for them to respect the children's demands. This will be an important function of the Laboratory, which should be carried out not only through conferences and publications but through concrete initiatives, proposals, activities.[7]

---

[7] See files n.6: "The reunion of the City commission government" and n.7: "The local police, a friend of the children".

Chapter 5

So that the children can go out alone

Let's return to our proposal – to assume the child as a parameter for the transformation of our cities. If we want to move forward from this general affirmation in an operational sense, we must make an important clarification. The condition of childhood in the world is strongly differentiated and oscillates between two extremes. On the one hand, the situation of the Western children, rich, metropolitan or, in any case, citizens, which is the one described above and that culminates in the pathological situation of loneliness. On the other, the situation of abandonment of children from poor societies, from the south of the world, from the great metropolises of South America. A situation that leads children to live alone, to suffer violence from adults, who see a danger in them or even just a hindrance. A situation of weakness and impotence that allows children to be exploited in inappropriate labor, or used as a non-punishable instrument of organized crime for sexual trafficking and even for organ transplantation. What the two situations have in common is the helplessness of the child in the respective societies and confirm the correctness of the proposal returning to the child precisely to reconstruct fairer, more human, more suitable societies for all. But surely both situations require a radically different assessment and solutions.[1]

Possible solutions are not ventured in these pages for the countries in the south of the world, which require knowledge and skills that the writer lacks. It is expected that others retake this stimulus by studying its appropriate application to those conditions. We continue, then, describing the possible concrete adaptations of the proposal in our cities of the western world, rich and consumerist. It must be said, however, that this privileged condition also contains a range of conditions that go from the village or the small town, where the effects of fear are still present to some extent, to the big city where the loneliness of the children is almost total, to the most degraded large suburbs

---

[1] On several occasions, and especially during the session of Permanent Peoples' Tribunal, held in Naples in 1995, and at conferences given in recent years in South America, I have had the opportunity to verify the interest in the general project proposed here, that is to say, to assume the child as a parameter of change, by representatives of countries of the south of the world, although much work must be done to be able to properly apply it to the specific needs of each social reality.

where, in our West, similar situations to those of the Third World can also be found, with children living on the street in a situation of abandonment.[2]

As proof of a correct application of this new philosophy of the city government, a specific objective, apparently small and simple, is indicated – that children can leave home alone.

Why is it so important to leave home?

For people like the one who writes this, who have had the possibility, probably the luck, of living their own childhood, especially outside of the home, among the ruins of houses bombarded by war, in the city alleys, in the cabin where the grandparents kept their tools, the temptation to say "that children can leave home alone *again*" is strong. But we are aware of how incorrect this nostalgic attitude is. The conditions in which our children grow up today are absolutely unprecedented, unparalleled with those of our childhood. And they are not new just because the feeling of neighborhood, solidarity and security has been lost, but above all, because social relations have become enormously more complex, distances have become wider. It is difficult to know each other, it is difficult to go down from the apartments on the highest floors, it is dangerous to cross the streets, etc. The city, however, has also become richer, more articulate and, if you like, more fascinating.

On the other hand, leaving home, walking the streets alone, knowing their environment, is an important requirement not only for the social but also the cognitive growth of the child. For us, adults, walking, going for a walk, is a pleasure, a gift that we often give ourselves; for children, on the other hand, it is a necessity. Our trips are, more and more often, transfers, steps from one point to another, aimed at a goal, therefore projected into the future, linked to a function. Distracted by these concerns, we try to reach the place of destination in the shortest possible time.[3] Children behave completely differently. They live their displacements as a succession of present moments, each important in itself, each worthy of a stop, a surprise, a contact. And then times are prolonged, children's pockets are filled with stones, sheets, papers, and the mind is filled with images, questions, new discoveries. And everything

---

[2] This book deals with the subject, limited to the Italian reality and specifically that of the street children of the historic center of Palermo. See the epigraph of the second part: "The street, a place of all" and the file n.19: "A stone garden".

[3] An effective example of these adult movements is the subway: a black tube between two stations. The route, the journey, no longer exists; only one starting point and one arrival point remain. The transfer time is wasted time and, therefore, should be as short as possible.

is together: the beautiful, the new, the general and the particular. And this is usually a cause of misunderstanding on the part of the adults who stubbornly recommend: "Do not stop all the time!", "Do not waste your time!", without realizing that it is precisely how, while wasting time, we grow older.[4]

It is unfortunate that the possibility of children going out, their autonomy, is inversely proportional to ours: the more we, adults, move by car, the more we widen our radius of movement and create dangers, obstruct the passage, pollute the air, and this increases the difficulties in the autonomy of our children. And when children move, it is more and more often in our company, inside our car, in the back seat. This means that the child does not see the city, fails to perceive its characteristics, passes quickly, cannot respond to the continuing need for the present, curiosity, making stops. It is dragged by us in an unnatural direction aimed at a goal. In this strange way of moving, it does not manage to understand anything, to organize its space, to build its city. Today's children often grow up with problems of spatial organization and with very low knowledge of their city, their neighborhood, their area.

Having their own experiences

The importance of free play in the development of a person has already been discussed. And free play implies autonomy, reuniting alone, free of control, with the possibility of facing one's own risk and thus experiencing the satisfaction of the solved problem, of the overcome difficulty.

In the past, children's time was clearly divided between the formal, the obligation, which was that of the school, homework, the catechism; and the informal, that of the pleasure, of play –"free time." The child autonomously administered this time and, if it did not transgress any of the social rules, it could get out of home, meet anyone it wanted, to devote him or herself to their favorite games. It was the time of personal experiences, which led girls and especially boys to explore their environment, to know its secrets,

---

[4] In a beautiful experience about the spatial organization of the youngest children, the educators at a Reggio Emilia nursery went out into the street, each time with a child, and took him back home, asking him to show them the way. An educator told me that when a child reached a corner, he had turned left and she had asked him to explain how he knew it was time to turn. The boy, with some stupor and after thinking a little, responded by pointing to the street: "Do you not see that paper there?" This means that the child knew where to turn, but had no reference points. He probably used a set of information that, together, said: "It's time to turn." But in the face of the adult's question, he could only indicate the paper as a reference.

observing the life of animals and plants, experiencing climatic changes, the characteristics of various elements of nature.

Today children's free time has disappeared. The dangers lurking outside the home advise against letting children go out alone and the best economic conditions allow their enrollment in many evening courses and activities: the pool, guitar, English, dance, the gym... "You should be grateful, nowadays you can know many things that we, when we were little, couldn't even have dreamed of!", we say to our children. Naturally, the most open parents make their children choose the afternoon courses they want to attend, so that the following eventual fatigue or the desire to leave them can be answered by arguing the economic reasons and even the noble causes of commitment and consistency: "You chose it". In reality, blackmail. If we add up the two trips to school planned in the schedule, the probable catechism lesson, two or three "voluntary" activities and homework, the child's afternoons are fully booked. There is an interval of one hour before dinner and it is usually taken up by television.

At the same time, mothers have become taxi drivers and spend the afternoon accompanying their children and waiting for them at the door of the gym, the pool, the church. And in the city of incommunicability, the new social micro groups of waiting mothers are formed, just as the group of those who take the dog out in the early morning or late afternoon is formed for the husbands.

A curious and disturbing reflection – if the organization of work continues with the current tendency, work schedules will tend to decrease more and more. The children of today, will be workers of tomorrow with much more free time compared to what we have nowadays; however, they will have been children without free time and, therefore, unable to use it, to take advantage of it. I fear that this may become a considerable opportunity within the reach of commercial production, which will offer ideas, instruments, manuals, entertainers for leisure time, the same way it offers them for children today, as games on their birthdays, for the family holidays...

The school, at least thus described by the good educators and the good teachers, should have been the place where the personal experiences of the students occurred, were elaborated until students and teachers obtained new knowledge together. This is the meaning of important teaching experiences such as the "free text" and the "collective text".[5]

Our school, at least at the official level, has almost completely absorbed these opinions and proposals, an absolute minority at the time when their authors launched them, adding them to the new programs. But if children live only collective experiences, organized and controlled by adults in the many courses they take, and the remaining time is absorbed by television, what experiences can the school work on? From what personal knowledge can the school activity start? Often the school, aware of this deficiency, proposes experiences, such as external visits, practical activities, in order to work on them later. But the suspicion that it only ends up creating a vicious circle is strong.

It is often heard that today's children do not say anything. Maybe because they have nothing to tell, because the adults who accompany them and watch them permanently know everything already! It is important then, that the child, from their first years, can go out alone, assuming the risk and pleasure of abandoning the domestic security; go down to the street, find a friend, play with them, agree on the game and its rules. Or experience nature with them, objects, comment on the behavior of the elderly; take risks together proportionate to their own strengths, overcoming obstacles, facing and resolving conflicts; return home tired, maybe dirty, excited, eager to tell what parents cannot know. This experience, whose complexity is undeniable from every point of view, and which should be had by all our children from the age of three or four, is possible today, perhaps for a boy older than ten and for a

---

[5] We refer to the proposal of the "free text" of Celestin Freinet carried out in Italy by the Movement for Cooperative Education (MCE) and of the "collective text". Free text means the voluntary writing of a short text that documents a fact, an experience that the student has lived outside of school and that it considers may interest his or her classmates. Each day, in class, a time is reserved for reading, discussion, and collective elaboration of free texts, the best of which are published later in the school newspaper. It is worth observing the profound difference between this proposal and that, still present, one of the "little thoughts." In this case, students are asked to write something (for example, ten thoughts about spring, about their mother or whatever comes to mind) without recipients (it would be absurd to read in class 200 or 250 trivial phrases), that will be corrected: precisely against every principle of communication. Collective text means the sum of personal contributions to collectively achieve a higher and more complex result that is no longer of one, but of all. Thus, was born *Letter to a teacher* (School of Barbiana, 1967) and several works within the MCE, for example, *The hot-air balloon*, a novel written in two years of Mario Lodi's elementary class (1972). On the collective creation text, see also the work of J. L. Corzo Toral (1983).

girl even later, when the period of great cognitive and social growth is already more than over. What consequences will this delay have on the child?

The domestic accidents

Another dramatic contradiction is that of accidents. We lock our children at home to protect them, although the house is by far the most dangerous place for them. More people die from domestic accidents than from street accidents. And those who suffer the most are the elderly and children, despite the fact that houses are now safer than they were yesterday and every year the assurances, safety standards, and obligations of builders are increased.

In the past, electric cables were external, water was often boiled in large quantities for cleaning and washing, floors were irregular, stairs were steep, and so on. Today these dangers no longer exist, but accidents increase.

The fact is that before we were at home the minimum time necessary, in order to eat, sleep, do homework, sometimes to help our mother, and, if anything, we went out to look for the risks. Today we spend too much time at home. The child must also stay there even when it has nothing to do, then it gets bored ... and a bored child is a child in danger! There is no security that can oppose the need to discover, to do, to play. Expressing little interest in the rooms where it usually spends too much time, the child cannot resist the temptation to put two pieces of wire inside the two fascinating holes of the plug or even to disassemble it, or to start the mixer, or to switch on the gas. If we leave alcohol, detergents and medication out of the child's reach, as recommended, and put them, for example, somewhere higher, we will get two negative results: first, that we will live less comfortably; second, that the danger of the products is increased by the child climbing on a chair placed on the table; because it will get to the bottles anyway. And they are always treacherous, uncontrollable dangers. On the other hand, the day that a child stops searching and taking risks will be a terrible one!

Today, home-security study programs are being promoted even internationally. I declare myself in absolute disagreement with these projects if they only serve to give us, adults, the peace of mind of being able to leave our children at home alone for even longer periods of time. And, on the other hand, the safer the house is, the more dangerous it will be, because the danger will not be expected, nor will it be predictable nor, therefore, controllable. If we really love our children, we must begin to defend them from the houses! We must act in such a way that children are not forced to stay at home more than necessary, that they can leave, that they can take risks to learn to defend themselves from dangers. Risk is a necessary component of development: a scratch on the knee, escape from an ambush by friends, run, jump, climb, but also pay attention to an approaching car, learning to measure the relationship between speed and distance, are all normal risks that a child can control, that help it grow.

In the face of the obsessive protection directed at children, a dramatic doubt arises: that all the risks that the child needed to take gradually, and which he had no chance to face, add up in some way until it becomes an unbearable urgency that explodes in the adolescence when young people can decide for themselves and then decide to play with death. This could be an interpretation of the suicide games of young people, such as the Russian roulette, crossing the intersections at full speed, lying on the dividing line of the lanes in the road at night...

The unsolvable conflict with television

Everyone is convinced that watching too much television is harmful and nobody knows what to do so that children do not abuse it. The most useful resource is strict regulation: "Only one hour a day", "Only a cartoon and a show", "If you turn it on now you will not be able to see your favorite program", and other phrases like that. These are sensible rules, but children cannot understand why they often have to turn off the television to do nothing. It means living in continuous conflict with their children which parents prefer to avoid so as not to compromise the little time they spend with them. We have another solution, much simpler, much less conflictive, suggested by the children themselves. Various investigations, including very recent ones, carried out in Italy and other countries, show that the vast majority of children put playing with their friends at the top of their wish list. Television generally appears in second place, and far behind.[6] It is enough to satisfy them, also in this case, as we so often do with their more foolish and uneducational whims. It is enough to find a way for children to go out, meet and play together, and thus we will also have solved this serious educational problem.

Also, with regard to television, as on the subject of the house, there is much talk about new solutions that point to better programming for children. Again, I strongly reiterate my disagreement. I do not want a better television if its purpose is to allow parents to leave their children in the arms of this comfortable "babysitter" for even more time, certain that they will only watch the good programs. Let us, instead, look for ways in which children can spend their free time playing with their friends outside the home and in that case, fighting for good television for children will be an alternative and it will be worth it. It may happen that among friends who are playing freely someone

---

[6] Oliverio Ferraris (1995).

says: "Today is Thursday, it's five o'clock, let's go home to see that show, it's worth it!"

Girls and boys

Not for reasons of principle, but simply of practical and consolidated habit, when I write I cannot use the feminine and masculine forms, that is, girl and boy, or the frightful mixed form[7]. I have always had the feeling that it is extremely uncomfortable to read such a written text, while it is acceptable to me in documents, manifestos, law texts. I trust it is not a final sexist resistance. I also thought of resorting to neutral forms such as childhood or " little one," but I always return, without much guilt, to the term "child", so concrete and familiar.[8]

Having said that, not to apologize, but at least as a clarification, I must recognize and make it clear that, nonetheless, the problem exists and is not easy to solve. When we say that children should be able to leave home alone, we have to be aware that we talk about girls and boys, and that when we have conveyed the principle that it is important and fair for boys to leave, it is not entirely true that applies for girls as well. It takes a lot of vigilance, appropriate and often creative proposals. The Children's Council of the Laboratory of Fano, for example, is rigorously formed, each school having to choose two representatives, a girl and a boy.

But obviously these are the easiest things to obtain; what is more difficult is to guarantee an effective autonomy to children of both sexes, to ensure that a father can in the same way, and with the same confidence, allow his daughter or son to leave home to meet their friends.

---

[7] In Spanish, *niñ/ao* can be used as a non-gender-specific term, same as in English "he/she". The whole idea in this subchapter is based on the notion that *niño* in Spanish can be used both to speak about boys and as a common term.

[8] When I draw (signing as FRATO), if I have to invent an image in which my characters appear and, for reasons of synthesis and emblematic representation, I cannot represent a boy and a girl, I often opt for a girl. A girl appears for example in the image of the Psychopedagogy Team of the CNR, a girl in the image of the Laboratory "Fano the city of children", in Palermo and in others. This freedom is allowed by the graphic language (nobody has ever asked me "Why is there only a girl and not a boy?"), but not the oral language and even less, the written. If I had titled the book "The City of Girls," everyone would have thought of a specific proposal for female children and not for everyone.

The child as an environmental indicator

Ecologists use environmental indicators, that is, those phenomena, those organisms, that help us check the health or degradation of our environment. Lichens, for example, modify their characteristics if the environment is contaminated, fireflies do not return there, nor do swallows, and so on. For the city, the child can be considered as a sensitive *environmental indicator*. If there are children who play in the city, who walk alone, it means that the city is healthy; if there are no children in the city, it means that the city is sick.

A city where children wander is a safe city, not only for them but also for the elderly, the disabled and for all citizens. Their presence represents a stimulus for other children to go down and a dissuasive factor for cars and other external dangers. The deserted street, however, is dangerous for the child who crosses it, because the driver does not expect it, cannot predict it. It is dangerous for everyone because it invites crime and makes it unpunished.

But to make it possible for children to leave home alone, the city must be changed, completely but gradually. The city, which has grown, wildly adopting the defense option, it must be able to offer alternatives, be open to life, open to the future. We must act, then, on several levels and in several directions.

Renegotiating the relationship of power between the car and the citizen

Huge amounts of money are being spent in favor of toads in many countries in northern Europe and North America. Yes, on toads. Highways are insurmountable barriers that fatally divide their territories. Thus, the poor toads can no longer pass from the aquatic reproduction environments to the humid ones of their habitual life. Or, in the cases where the fences allow them to pass, they are forced to cross the highways with a very low percentage of success. Consequently, a cry of protest has been raised and the societies that built or managed the highways had no choice but to open connection tunnels between the two sides of the highway every certain number of meters. Naturally, this has a very high cost, but it saves the lives of many toads and allows them to traverse the territory. I show solidarity with the toads and I completely agree with these actions for their preservation. I just wish that the same attention and sensitivity were dedicated to children. Their territory is also cut by roads where the rights of the cars dominate. Crossing them is dangerous, parents worry and prevent their children from traveling alone. Thus, children cannot reach their friends or, together with them, reach the places where they can play – the playground, the open field, the avenue.

The physical barrier becomes a psychological and cognitive barrier, it limits the child's sphere, it limits its spatial and affective development. It is as if the child had half of its toys removed, half of the television darkened, half of the textbook torn out.[9]

In today's city, a walk is an adventure: sidewalks occupied by parked cars or commercial stalls, chaotic traffic, disrespect for the priority of pedestrians at zebra crossings. If it is difficult for everyone, it is even more difficult for weaker citizens such as the elderly, the disabled, the children. Under these conditions, the use of the car, considered a protective structure, is almost an act of self-defense, with known consequences: traffic congestion, transformation of public land into private space, air pollution, noise pollution, vibrations that endanger the monuments.

Let's imagine that there are some cars parked on both sides of a street and suppose that car A is double parked on the left, while car B is parked on the right, across the sidewalk, which makes it difficult or impossible for pedestrians to pass by. If the local police tow truck arrives, it is most likely that car A would be taken and it is possible that car B would not even be fined. What does this mean? That it is dealt with decisively and with a firm hand if the parking hinders the movement of cars; that there is greater tolerance if those disadvantaged are the pedestrians, therefore the weakest. However, a disabled person who moves in a wheelchair or a mother who pushes a stroller may not be able to continue their journey. A child or an elder may be forced to get off the sidewalk and expose themselves to unnecessary dangers.

Cars are, in fact, the new masters of the city; solutions and ease are studied for them, the most radical and expensive operations are carried out in their favor. Think of the plans for new car parks in big cities. It is for them that the local police spend most of their time and energy. The fines that apply are mostly for parking in prohibited spaces, that is to say, for a crime that causes more harm to the movement of the cars themselves, and relatively little to the people. Cars, in motion or stopped, permanently occupy a considerable percentage of public land by transforming it into private space – almost all streets and squares have become parking lots. When it is proposed to restore public space to citizens, the most frequent response is: "First, the parking problem has to be solved and then we can think about a social use of the square". This seems to me like an incorrect reasoning. Having space to "support" the car itself is, without a doubt, a necessity, but I don't think it can be considered a right – when a citizen acquires a car, the mayor does not commit himself to reserve a public-space area for it to be driven or parked.

---

[9] Interesting is the study of the setbacks in the socio-cognitive development of children caused by the urban barriers imposed by dangerous crossroads (Bonanomi, 1994).

Being able to move calmly on foot and use public space, however, is undoubtedly a right of all citizens. Restoring the possibility of moving freely on foot to everyone is, therefore, an imperative duty of the administrator and a correct and serious way to plan the future of the city. A future in which the power of cars ends where pedestrian rights begin; a future in which the city is cleaner, less "busy", where we can move; where we can meet; where, in short, we can live better. Where it is possible for a child to leave home alone and play with its friends. So, first of all, the square will be restored to the citizens; then, if possible, a solution for the problem of parking will be sought.

When the pedestrian zones are safe, developed, respected,[10] and also introduced into the suburban residential neighborhoods, it will be necessary to distinguish and treat them differently, both during the project and when in use; the streets of the cars (those of great movement, in which the pedestrians must accept the conditions of the cars) from the streets of the pedestrians (those which the cars can access, but under the conditions that the pedestrians impose). This urban rethinking, already in motion in many cities in central and northern Europe, should tend not so much to create new and stricter prohibitions, but to make speed and danger impossible. Parents will not overcome their fear because the speed limit has been reduced from 50 to 30 kilometers per hour, because they can always and justly think about the possible violation of the rules and therefore refuse to recognize their child's autonomy. But, if the lane of the street is restricted and becomes tortuous or blocked by obstacles, speed will be impossible and adults may be calmer and more permissive.

A good example of structural intervention in favor of pedestrians is the "sidewalk that crosses the street" – a pedestrian crossing that maintains both the level and paving of the sidewalk. While the pedestrian is normally the one who "gets off" the sidewalk, leaving his safe territory, and enters the dangerous one of the cars, in this case, the pedestrian remains in his territory and it is the car that, by means of a ramp "goes up" onto the pedestrian crossing, invading an area that is not its own and consequently having to worry about possible pedestrians.

If speed is impeded, the street is safer, not only because it reduces the danger of traffic but also because it becomes more difficult to even commit a crime – it is difficult to escape, there are more people walking, there is more social control.

---

[10] It would be desirable that the administrators, local-police officers, the civil guard, also respect the pedestrian zone (at least in small and medium-sized cities), traveling on foot or by bicycle and thus sending a consistent message to the other citizens.

Help the adults understand that children need to go out

Adults are afraid, and they do not lack reasons to be, but, as said before, the defense has no hope and future. Locking children at home means exposing them to the danger of domestic accidents, entrusting them to the television and depriving them of fundamental experiences. But overcoming fear is difficult and words are not enough to achieve it. Governors must take care of these problems and help their fellow citizens. We have to work at different levels: first of all, help parents understand that children need free time, need to handle themselves and take their own risks, rather than do many things and take part in many courses in the afternoon; then help them regain confidence in their children's capability, which is surely greater than they imagine. It is necessary to help parents get out of the individualistic and defensive perspective, thinking that all children must be together outside the home and that all adults should be a point of reference and safety for children. It is necessary, however, to reduce the environmental danger by decreasing the speed of traffic, favoring the movements of pedestrians and bicycles, firmly applying those rules that punish those who do not respect the rights of pedestrians.

Adults must be helped to understand that a good parent is not one who gives up their own life so that their children can have everything and can be accompanied to the different schools in the morning and classes in the afternoon. The first characteristic of a "good parent" should be to become less and less necessary for their own child. When a child is born, perhaps the most important moment is the significant and profound transformation that occurs in a few minutes: the cutting of the umbilical cord. From that moment on, the child separates from the mother and can start its relationship with her and, through her, its relationship with the world – the great adventure of autonomy. Each day the separation can be confirmed and consolidated, or denied; we can become less indispensable for our children and thus help them to distance themselves from us, or do the opposite and tie new umbilical cords.

I think that a second characteristic of a "good parent" is that of being a good adult model. An adult that makes the child think it is worth getting older to be like them or to find people like them. A serene adult, able to surrender, happy. One that tries to realize their aspirations, cultivate their passions, live their sexuality well, live their profession, ideals, beliefs, with dedication, with strength and consistency. This is not only valid in the relationship between parents and children, but also between teachers and students and in general between adults and children. I think this is a rewarding perspective, which invites us to serenity and surrender, and to have even happier children.

A serene and accomplished adult will know how to understand their child's need for autonomy and be willing to overcome any difficulty, any concern to be able to secure it.

Find new allies for children

A few decades ago, children were "everyone's". The neighborhood functioned as a great social control. If a child, while playing outside the house, needed something, it would find a curious, attentive and worried eye in the neighbors. I remember that if, playing with friends, I did something I shouldn't have done (I fought, I hit someone, I fell ...), when I returned home, I found reproach or punishment, even before I could say what happened. We had no phone, but evidently, the news had already been spread "with haste"! This was common in the small town where everyone knew each other, but also in the big city where the neighborhood allowed for a daily relationship of its inhabitants, for work, for shopping, for school, always close to home. But the criterion of social responsibility with respect to the child was even broader than knowing or being neighbors – a child away from home, especially if it was alone, was controlled and protected by the adults he encountered. More than neighbors of the home, one could say they were neighbors of the child. And this "neighborhood" grew over the years, it extended as the child's autonomy developed and allowed for more daring expeditions in new, unexplored territories. There, it also found interested and worried adults. This naturally favored growth, the discovery of new spaces, the possibility of new adventures that built and consolidated new knowledge.

Now, this social solidarity seems lost. The defense option has inhibited the interest in others, or at least has hidden it, masked it. The immediate temptation is to lock yourself in safe places: the house, school, different evening courses. And the requirements of other spaces grow, perhaps freer, but always protected and guarded: libraries, laboratories, gardens with gates and guarded entrances.[11]

The loss of autonomy produces resignation, but also discontent and discomfort. A desire and willingness for solidarity survives, which is reflected in the interested reactions in proposals such as this one: they must be taken out, allowed to become experiences. We, however, cannot wait for this diffusion of solidarity to be reconstructed to guide the experiences we are talking about –

---

[11] For this purpose, it is interesting to analyze the differences between the urban spaces "playground" and "sandbox" (Bozzo, 1995).

children are in a hurry, they are children for only a few years. Therefore, we must identify and train the new allies of children as soon as possible.

The local police

Cities have a small army that exhausts its energies in being almost exclusively at the service of cars. This confirms the power of the car in our society and, with the current lack of social sensitivity and solidarity, it seems a waste and even degradation of a presence that could be much more significant and qualified. We propose that the local police officers also become, perhaps imperatively, children's friends. When a child is in a difficult situation, seeing a policeman should calm the child down, assure it that the person in uniform will solve its problem. What needs, what difficulties can a child face? It may want to pee and be ashamed to enter a bar and ask; it may be thirsty; it may have been late and need to call home and has no money; it may be bothered by an adult; it may have fought with a friend; it may be lost; it may have fallen and injured its knee; it may have lost its bus ticket to return home. Each of these situations represents a suffering, a great suffering as are the sufferings of children the majority of the time. The local police should have the institutional duty to help children who are in compromised or distressing situations. They will have to solve its problem, accompanying the child to a bar so it can drink water, pee, call someone, or offer it a bus ticket. It would be important that this social role of the local police officers is made public and suitably disseminated so that both children and their parents know of it. If we really want to increase the autonomy of children, we must reduce the fears of their parents and all adults.

As it has been said several times, that the police are a friend of the children also means they are a point of reference for the elderly, for the handicapped, for the lady who comes back loaded with shopping bags. Being friends with children means, in short, being friends with the citizens. For this new and important social function, agents must be prepared, by opening different stages of training and debate that define new objectives and behaviors.[12]

One could think of extending this social function of "friends of children" to all those who wear a uniform and, therefore, are easily recognizable. The mayor could invite the local police, employees of security companies and firefighters, as well as public-transport drivers or cleaners, to take on this new role to help make the city more suitable for citizens, starting with the children. For this, organized training and awareness is needed.

---

[12] On this point, see file n.7: "The local police, a friend of the children."

The elderly

Today our rich society is aging. As there are few children and life is being prolonged, the "alarm" of the elderly is born. According to the latest statistics, there are three grandparents for each grandchild, too many retirees with respect to the number of workers. There are, in short, too many old people and we do not know where to put them, what to do with them, how to take care of them. In a consumerist society like ours, every need produces suitable articles. As a result, television commercials promoting products to the elderly are born, from woolen garments to products to attach dentures. In a city founded on division and specialization, every need, every discomfort, suggests adequate services. Homes for the elderly, schools for the elderly, organized trips, and day centers are born.

Again, answers designed not for their natural recipients, but for adult citizens, for those who must care for the elderly, for the strong citizens. An elder does not like being with the elderly. The elder has the most important heritage in his history, in his past, in his memory; he has, therefore, a great desire to tell stories.[13] He is not interested in listening and learning because he knows he has no future in which to invest. Putting ten elders together is creating a paradoxical situation, against nature: everyone will want to tell stories, but no one will be interested in listening. An old man makes sense in the middle of the other generations, among children and young people who want to listen and learn. Ten elders together can speak only of the coming death. Those tourist trips are pathetic for the elderly, those coaches that unload them in winter on deserted beaches (they say that the sea air is good for the elderly, especially during winter!), between closed hotels, with gray hair in the wind, meaningless 'Fellinian' scenes which carry a lot of sadness.

There are unions, sports, cultural, recreational associations, even universities for the elderly. I don't agree; I don't think it's fair. Again, the separation and specialization: the elderly are a special reality, with their problems that require specialized answers such as the claim of pensions, exercise, dancing, meetings, always for the elderly. A Sunday cycling club should be open to men and women, children, adults and the elderly. And when the elder does not feel able to pedal with the others, he can teach how to take care of a bicycle, give advice to the younger members, make the children dream by narrating their experiences. Instead of organizing a club of former cyclists who tell their sorrows or go for tricycle rides. The important thing is to

---

[13] An African said: "For us, the elderly are very important, because they are like traveling libraries."

be elderly along with those who are not, to continue making sense. Men also like to be with women and children with the elderly!

We must learn to think that what we consider as the "alarm" of the elderly can become their " solution."

The elder lives a very particular period of life: their expectations, the desire to excel, and the need to compete are over. A period that could be serene, selfless, free, if the elder was not forced to sadly reflect for the other elders or lose himself in his future death in solitude. The calmness, the happiness of the old person, is linked to the illusion that their experience can serve someone, that they can still be useful for something, that all the time they have left, can be as important as that already spent. Thus, arises the elder, the grandparent, as the privileged ally of children.

It may be refuted that the elderly are often bad tempered, do not want to be behind the children. This is true and they have the right to it, but we have so many elders that there will undoubtedly be a few who are good contributors. On the other hand, I do not believe that the elderly can or should be asked to adopt particular roles or responsibilities. I think they should be asked to refuse isolation at home, to go out, to "be." That they be present in the gardens, in the open meeting places, in the streets; that they live in the neighborhood, that they share it with the other citizens and especially with the children, with the handicapped, so that it is more habitable and safer for all. Their presence will give security to the children.

These are social background options: the house, the street, the gardens, the neighborhood, instead of the Senior Center or the retirement home. Options that should be provided by the State, local institutions, associations. It means investing energy so that the elderly can remain in their environment, with their relatives, with their neighbors, with children, rather than investing in expensive organizations of detention and marginalization. If the elderly feel accepted, useful, necessary, they will be better, they will be more autonomous, they will make the city safe. It will be a great saving of money and a fitting demonstration of affection and recognition towards those who have come before us.

The merchants

Vendors, artisans, and shopkeepers, are not necessarily good and patient, nor are they available to children. In order to obtain a license, they do not have to demonstrate special didactic or educational qualities, but they share a very peculiar and important condition for our discourse: "they are in the street". And while the local police and the elderly may not be within reach of the child at certain times, the stores are always there and can represent a safe place. In relation to what we said before about the new insecurities and fears, vendors can rebuild a network of safety and reference. They can offer a simple answer to the question: "But if something happens to my child, who can it go to?" If all the vendors, artisans, as well as banks and post branches, declared themselves available to ensure the autonomy of the children, put an allusive poster on their window, the children and their parents could be calmer because they would know that, if necessary, these are points of reference.[14] The vendor will keep an eye on the passing child. The child can ask the shopkeeper to call home without paying, pee, drink a glass of water, be comforted if something has happened to it.

We have pointed out some possible allies of children, but we must also teach them that each adult is a potential friend. We must abandon the terrorist recommendations: "Do not talk to anyone", "Do not ask anyone for anything", and instead teach them that, when they need something, they go to an adult and ask for help. This will not only be a small contribution to educate children on how to live in this world and live in it as well as possible, but it will also be a strong wake-up call for adults, who are already numbed by indifference and general selfishness.

---

[14] On this point, see file n.9: "Let's go to school alone."

Chapter 6

A city suitable for children

Children being able to leave the house unaccompanied is an important goal, given the current disordered and disrespectful development of the city; however, this does not preclude the change that today's city requires.

The city, grown almost against the needs of its inhabitants, especially the weakest, must review all its structures and plans to make it suitable for all. That is why it is worth continuing the challenge, the provocation of taking the child as a parameter of change, and insisting on the idea that when the city is more suitable for children it will be more suitable for all.

Not being able to analyze all the facets of a city in detail here, we will give only examples. In the third part of the book, through the files, we will try to enter more operatively in the proposals, in the activities, in the initiatives.

The beautiful city[1]

Italy is famous in the world for its cities. Our ancestors dedicated energy, resources, ingenuity and creativity to make the places where their life, their work, was spent, where they educated their children, where they loved each other, spent their old age, where they died, beautiful. This beauty is also evident by the fact that our country owns more than 60% of the works of art from around the world and that people from the farthest countries arrive to visit our cities and wander their streets.[2] Is the apparent contemporary suspicion that all this has happened because our ancestors had nothing more important to do really sustainable? Or is it that we are losing the meaning of life more believable? We rush, we certainly do more things and more quickly than our predecessors, but then we have the "right" to (not only need for) vacations, we maintain an army of psychologists, we consume frightening amounts of psychiatric drugs.

---

[1] The architect Cervellati will excuse me for borrowing the title of his book (*The beautiful city*).

[2] It is useful to reflect on the feeling of beautiful our ancestors had, certainly less educated than us and destined for a life harder than ours. They turned, carved and decorated the handles of their work instruments, painted the cars they would use in their life of hard work with flowers and exotic scenes.

Our cities are full of churches, monuments, palaces, fountains, sacred buildings, defined paving, games of light, of perspectives. When going through them, we are always exposed to surprise, to admiration. They invite us to stop and admire, pray, find someone. In short, cities are journeys. It is easily predictable that the child who walks these streets will also be enriched on a cognitive level. They were cities designed to be traveled on foot, because only by walking can those details, those beautiful corners be appreciated. And today, as the citizens privileged with these splendors, what do we do?

If possible, we try to go under these wonders – the dream of the contemporary citizen is the subway. If this is not possible, we try to pass over these wonders or, in any case, pass quickly. Thus, the viaducts, the beltways, the fast-moving roads are born. If these solutions are not possible due to the city's ridiculously narrow and winding streets and with its anachronistic monuments, then we try to move inside a motorized box that prevents us from stopping, admiring, surprising ourselves.

The fact that the car is the new master of the city leads to a number of consequences, including the cultural, the once important. When going by car, the beauties of the city lose value because they are not noticed, they are not seen. When going at fifty kilometers per hour and having to be attentive to traffic, you cannot perceive the foreshortenings, the perspectives, the details that great artists have also made for us in the past centuries. But it is not just this.

Cars have their "idea" of the city, their own aesthetics, and they are imposing it on us. It is an aesthetic profoundly different from ours. It is that of garages (individual or collective, underground or over ground, as a large underground warehouse over several floors...), of gas stations (always very bright, very large and all the same), of road signs, of billboards (simple and too large to be seen in progress). It is that of asphalt (less noisy than paving), of crash barriers (safer). It is that of the horns and the burglar alarms (even when they wake the children up and cause fear). It is that of car cemeteries, which are building a final macabre ring around our beautiful cities and our ugly outskirts. When the conflict was evident between drivers' safety and the right to continued life of the trees and poplar groves (also of great importance to the aesthetic, landscape and health of the city) no doubt was cast, no alternatives were explored such as the diversion of the roads of the decrease in speed – the trees were simply cut down.

The open conflict between the aesthetics of cars and that of people, at least as our ancestors expressed it, is evidenced by the fact that in these last fifty years, cars have damaged the cities' monuments with pollution and vibrations more than fires, wars and earthquakes in the past centuries and millennia would have been able to. Finally, the overwhelming desire for the prominence of the car should be noted. It is practically impossible to see or photograph a corner of our cities without a car "in the view." There is no pedestrian zone or holiday period free of them: a car, even that of the local police or the deputy or the diplomat, will prevent you from seeing a street or a monument in the way that its artist originally conceived or designed.

Nobody wants to give up the car. I think it is a sensible duty to renegotiate its relationship, and our own, with the city. The city will be beautiful again only when it is possible to travel on foot again. Today, trips are transfers from point to point, as quickly as possible. We must feel the pleasure of tours again. If we, the adults, do not have time for these frivolities, that is unfortunate, but let's not deprive our children, our elders and all those foreign adults who come to visit our cities from this pleasure, this need. If it is possible to rove the city on foot again, our urban planners, our architects, our artists, must again be concerned with surprising, gratifying, accompanying their fellow citizens through the streets.[3] It will then be important to return space to the footpath,

---

[3] In 1995 a national congress on slowness was held in Florence titled: *The world has time to lose*, organized by the COOP (Consumers' Cooperative). In my intervention, "Who still wants to waste time with the children?", I began with these reflections: to go from Rome to Florence you can travel along the Cassia road. This does not only represent a transfer, but it means crossing towns and small cities, different landscapes, seeing, and discovering. It means stopping, delaying and accelerating, being surprised and angry. This requires time, but it is not wasted time. On that trip there is more than just moving, there is pleasure. It is necessary to take time in the villages, collect their images, their rumors, their habits. Stop to eat their products and their typical dishes. It is possible to eat *finocchiona* (sausage seasoned with fennel), *spaghetti* with hare, white beans, wash them down with the red wine of Montalcino or with the Nobile wine of Montepulciano. It means approaching and moving away with respect to a landscape that changes, following the strange zigzags of the road, designed more for the encounter than for the rush, going up and down according to the gentle undulations of the Tuscan hills. Also, going from Rome to Florence, you can instead use the highway of the Sun and then the experience will be different. The main function of the highway is the point-to-point displacement, from toll to toll, with the least possible number of distractions and impediments; kill the time, allow the speed. The highways are all the same, the gas stations are all the same, and all equally efficient and fast; just as the food houses are the same; you can eat a *panino fattoria* anywhere in the Italian geography. Faced with a natural obstacle, the highway prefers to go underground or by air, rather than follow the "diversities" of the terrain: you don't have to get distracted, you don't have to slow down, you don't have to waste time. Indeed, the time is less, but it has been lost. In short, it only serves to move.
I have a similar feeling when I choose the plane instead of the train, for example, on the Rome-Milan trip. The flight time is obviously much shorter, but the trip as a whole varies little: from three hours or three and a half hours by plane to four hours by train.

take care of the paving of the sidewalks, restrict the streets, create rest areas, meeting places, return the squares to the people and children's play. In short, there will be much to do for cities to regain their beauty.

Some people think that these projects are luxuries that we cannot afford. This would be true if we were so cynical as to give up our artistic heritage. If so, we can effectively let our monuments be ruined and adopt without regret the new city of cars, speed, noise, pollution. "In spite of everything", we are not, we are not able to get rid of our works of art and we invest huge sums in restoration works, increasingly frequent, expensive and desperate. If we tried to eliminate the causes of this degradation, we would make not only culturally fair, but also economically advantageous choices.

Then there is the great problem of the suburbs, which are not characterized by their beauty, but still, we cannot demolish them. But if this awareness increases with respect to the rights of the citizens, from the smallest and the weakest, if the right to live in the city, to travel through it, to meet and have fun is recognized, then it will be necessary to think that our suburbs also have the right to be beautiful. It is a magnificent challenge that the administrators must give to architects, to urban planners, based on the awareness that the suburbs are potentially good and must be made suitable for children, with their spaces not yet resolved, with their natural corners forgotten by the blind urbanization. All spaces not yet constructed should be used to restore them to social use. Suburban pedestrian areas must be created; liberate the squares, if there are any, and return them to the citizens; create squares where they are not planned. The old industrial structures (factories, furnaces, warehouses) can be rehabilitated and converted into spaces for public use. We will have to think about the sidewalks, the monuments, the fountains. It will be a matter, in short, of facing a great social and aesthetic rehabilitation project of the suburbs. In this great project, children have much to say and give, because "reasonable" options are no longer enough; it is necessary to dare, invent, find new ideas that, by the way, children are not lacking.

The General Urban Plan

The commitment to revise and transform the city starting from the child can cover both large-scale interventions, such as the General Urban Plan or the Circulation Plan, as well as small projects linked to the opportunities for children to play, walk; and meeting and resting opportunities for adults

---

But the hours by plane are lost hours, fragmented in many different and short routes, in many procedures; while train hours are all good: to read, to write, to draw.

around their homes. By adopting the child's perspective, many of the city's major problems are seen more clearly and out of the ambiguities of the adult debate that is currently underway.

Naturally, we do not intend to discuss these technical matters with the competence of the urban planner. We just want to continue to consistently apply this new perspective to the analysis of the city and the proposal for change. Conceiving a new urban plan means redesigning the city. If the city recognizes the right of citizenship to all its citizens, the urban plan should be a mirror of this option.[4] Designing a city that is more suitable for children means designing the most beautiful, most habitable and, therefore, most suitable for everyone.

A city custom-made for children

In recent decades, the dimensions of the cities have increased enormously, too quickly; therefore, without a reflexive and programmed development, but rather guided by especially speculative reasons and hence without aesthetic or social concerns. The city has become huge and dangerous without creating new identities, new belongings.

First of all, the possibility of recognizing the city itself and recognizing ourselves in the city must be returned to the citizen, starting from the children. A dimension compatible with the knowledge and control skills of the citizens, and especially the children, must be returned to the cities. From this point of view, the adoption of the metropolitan area project that subdivides the metropolis into several municipalities that do not exceed one hundred or one hundred and fifty thousand inhabitants, which could correspond to the current district, is correct and pressing. Each City Council must have the characteristics of a local institution.

- *Autonomy.* A City Hall, with its name, its headquarters, its mayor, its Municipal Council. Owner of all the rights the Town Halls currently have and, hopefully soon, of all those tax transfers and government powers that the State will pass to the cities. The most appropriate headquarters, at least in

---

4 When I first met the mayor of Palermo, who urged me to accept the task of advising on the project "The city of children" in his city, he asked me to work together with the architect Cervellati, who was preparing the new Urban Plan from Palermo because, from this plan and the decisions that follow, it could be understood that the city had chosen the children. It seems to me a beautiful cultural challenge and a great commitment to the possibilities of this new government philosophy.

our culture and with respect to our history, of a genuine decentralization. Then, we must find a way to manage the metropolis, associating the different municipalities for all common interests or for all projects that go beyond the municipalities. There are foreign experiences that deserve to be studied and there are our management experiences, for example of roads, that go from municipal to provincial and state competencies, depending on the involved territories and agencies.

- *Identity.* In each of the metropolitan municipalities, urban and architectural solutions must be proposed that favor a feeling of identity of the population: to recreate a citizen center, the squares, the headquarters of the public offices, the monuments, places of meeting, of exhibitions, of shows. Naturally, it will be important that those in charge of these actions take the traditions seriously, the natural transformations of the places and value their monuments, from the most illustrious and well-known of the historical centers to the areas of industrial archeology of the suburbs, linked to the social history of the neighborhoods and the city. It is also worth highlighting the difficulty of developing a suitable spatial organization in children who have grown up in the anonymous and deprived suburbs of strong environmental indicators, in comparison to their peers who grew up in the historical centers.[5] This means that the ugly city also causes cognitive pathologies (in addition to social) and that, if this occurs in children, the suburban populations will build their future accordingly based on these limitations, adding one difficulty after another.

- *Accessibility.* An important principle of democratization must be affirmed: that all citizens can reach the places of their competency and their interest alone. This makes the citizen autonomous and free. In particular, it is important to guarantee children their autonomy to leave home, go play with friends and go to school on their own; guarantee routes without barriers and a solution of continuity to those with disabilities;

---

[5] Lynch, 1960; Bonnes, Rullo, 1995.

guarantee pedestrian walkways and safe crosswalks for the elderly to go to collect their pension, to go shopping, to the cinema, to the church, and so on. It is important to ensure to all citizens a real possibility of movement, of going to school, to work, to have fun, with other means than the private car, first of all on foot and by bicycle.

An urban plan of mobility

If the city should be more accessible, then we cannot commit to a mobility plan, because in this case we are already inside a car and we will end up interpreting and facing all the problems from the point of view of the motorist. The stated objective of mobility plans is, in general, to make traffic more fluid and faster. Their usual solutions are to widen the streets, make them straight, install smart traffic lights, adopt one-way roads, and so on. These are all measures that do not usually achieve the expected result but that make life more difficult and uncomfortable for those who do not use a car.

They do not get the expected result because in our cities less than half of the cars owned by citizens are in use, on average. The other half remains in the garages, in the parking lots, because they are not worth moving: traffic is too slow, parking is difficult to find and the risk of fines is high. In the city, then, there is a "reserve army" waiting for the conditions to be more favorable in order to get moving. If it is then possible to make the traffic of the cars more fluid, the parking easier, even if it is paid, that "reserve army" will move. After the changes, for a few days, it will appear as if satisfactory results have been achieved in the movement of vehicles, but as the number of cars increases, the benefits will be in vain. We will once again have a collapse in the circulation, but with a much higher percentage of cars meaning the solutions will become more difficult or even impossible. And after all this, the conditions for pedestrians and cyclists, which has never been taken into account, will have worsened significantly. This is not the catastrophic forecast of a pessimist; it is the confirmation of many countries which have carried out, and later abandoned, these suicide policies.

We must think instead of an urban mobility plan, based on the right that all citizens have to move freely and safely in their urban space, which is public land. The city must be returned to the citizens, a category that includes those who, such as children, the elderly, the disabled and many housewives, are only pedestrians. They do not need harsher laws, but a city made differently, with sidewalks on all streets, totally free of cars, merchandise and traffic signs, from which you can easily step off. Streets that can be crossed without difficulty and without danger and with pedestrian areas in the suburb neighborhoods also.

If we really want our cities to become lighter, we must favor alternative mobility systems over that of the motor. Particular attention should be given to cycling journeys, as long as the characteristics of the city permit it.

Bicycle lanes cannot be limited to being areas of the street separated from car lanes only by yellow stripes or curbs, because they are unsafe, because they are unhealthy when exposed to the fumes of the exhaust pipes (you will never give up the car if it is healthier and safer than the bicycle). The "bikeway" is not only intended for occasional sports activities, but as a true alternative to cars in urban mobility to go to school, to work, to go shopping. Therefore, a network of bicycle lanes has to be designed, taking some streets from the cars, passing through the parks, on the banks of the rivers, behind the railroad tracks. Reserved, protected, safe, short streets (the longest routes for cars, which "tire" less) and as clean as possible.

If we really are a democratic society, the urban mobility plan must take into account a hierarchy of needs based on those of the weakest, that is, pedestrians first and then cyclists; then the means of public transport and finally the private means. Without sectarianism, but with a clear idea of priorities.

If mobility becomes the main objective, the instruments for carrying it out must be as indicated below:

- *Reduce the speed of car traffic when it affects residential areas.* The legal limits are not enough; structural conditions that impede greater speed must be created: maximum lane restriction, two-way driving, avoid very straight lines that lead to increased speed.

- *Favor the pedestrian routes.* When conflicts and incompatibility between the rights of pedestrians and those of cars arise, those of pedestrians will always be guaranteed, primarily. Closely linked to this point is the "Let's go to school alone" project, which wants to be an educational approach to a different modality of thinking about mobility in future generations.

- *Encourage bicycle tours by decisively assigning some streets only to cycling traffic.* The apparent damage to the circulation of cars will be compensated by the lower number of circulating vehicles if an increasing number of citizens adopt this mode of transport. The "Let's go to school alone" project for middle school should be precisely and primarily aimed at the use of the bicycle.

- *Reduce and decentralize parking.* If you want to increase the quality of the historic center or the residential areas, we must prevent the passage of cars. In order for this objective to be attainable, the installation of car parks in the center must be critically rethought, as their presence attracts cars, and decentralizes them by educating people to reach the center only by public means, by bicycle or on foot.

- *Make the means of public transport competitive.* In this new scenario of lighter, cleaner and quieter city, the problem of public means must be reconsidered. Public means are also suitable for all citizens and therefore easily accessible, with entrances at sidewalk level, quiet, ecological, punctual and with reserved lanes. In short, it will be faster, more comfortable and cheaper to move by alternative means than by private car. The citizen is not dumb and always chooses to follow economic criteria. If you can move easily with alternative means you will gladly leave your car in the garage.

- *Educate by example.* It will be important, finally, that also the local agents and the police in charge of the urban area are moving on foot or by bicycle.

Our administrators are today called to an important and encouraging election. They should put their possibilities into practice with the conviction that, by speeding up the mobility of pedestrians and bicycles, and the public, the use of private means of transport will be inclined to slowly but regularly decrease. This means not investing in work that makes traffic more fluid, in the widening of lanes, in the installation of intelligent traffic lights... It means, instead, investing in sidewalks, in safe crossings, in bicycle lanes, in decreasing the traffic speed limit. And many countries in central and northern Europe are doing so with significant results.[6]

Repopulate the historic center

The historic center of the cities is a place where children could live well thanks to the pedestrian areas, squares and courtyards, gardens, monuments,

---

[6] In Copenhagen, the free loan of thousands of bicycles is being experimented at various stations or stops. The citizen can take a bicycle at one station and, after having used it, leave it at another, the one that is most comfortable for him.

fountains and the same urban structure that lends itself well to pedestrian travel and children's games. On the other hand, today, it is difficult for young couples to marry and have children due to the lack of housing. A firm commitment could be made to recover the largest number of publicly owned areas and buildings in the historic center, dilapidated, unused or misused, and allocate them to popular construction to allocate apartments preferably to young couples. Taking children to the center of the cities will be an action of great civic value, taking with them the life, the commotion of games. Another category that could be favored by such commitment is that of the elderly, who could regain their own autonomy in the center, which they fatally lose in the suburban neighborhoods due to the distance, height of buildings and lack of stimuli. The elderly and children are made precisely to be together and the center of a city is the best place for them to meet, for their involvement.

Give up the playgrounds to the children

The spaces for children to play, separated and specialized, are rigorously the same in all our cities and around the world, and their goal, as we said before, is not to meet the children's playing requirements but to respond to the concerns of the adults. To do this, the architect not only defines the area but also presumably indicates the types and modalities of games with which a child can entertain itself there. If we try to remember which were the best places for our children's games,[7] we will notice with surprise that they were the ones "not fit" for the adults. I think of the stairs, of the stairwell, of the sidewalk, of the bombed houses in the city, of the tool shed, of the slope between the road and the field. They were also, almost always, forbidden places, where we were looking for the risk, to have fun and grow older.

All of this is also valid today, as numerous studies and research show: children do not like rigidly defined, separate, dedicated spaces. They prefer adaptable spaces, usable in different ways according to the demands of the game.[8] They often prefer to share adult spaces, inventing new and creative ways to use them. Think, for example, of how children who are lucky enough to have their own room from their earliest years (once again a separate and specialized space) systematically refuse to use it as a play space and prefer

---

[7] I have said several times that it is not right to go back to the past because the experience offered to our children is absolutely new and requires new proposals and solutions, but if it is true that the children have lost many of the possibilities of playing then, it may be useful to examine the conditions and characteristics of our childhood games, at least to "find the way back".
[8] See bibliographic references on «The game and the urban environment».

instead to play in the kitchen where their mother is busy, even inventing fantastic environments under the table or around the sink.

The real problem is that adults are not able to provide spaces for children's play; and if we really want to respond to their needs, instead of dedicating or designing spaces we must learn to leave spaces. Leaving spaces does not mean giving up designing them; instead, it means doing it in a different way, with more humility, with more generosity, with more creativity, believing that the children know how to play, what to play and with whom to play. Leaving spaces means gifting. This means that in the design of the city, the spaces dedicated to children must disappear and provide instead spaces that are rich, common, nearby, original, open to all, suitable for children and the elderly, for whoever wants to read the newspaper and for lovers. Rich spaces means articulated, lively, with obstacles, weeds, walls, trees, diverse materials. Spaces where everyone can do what they want, because they are not for single use, they are not spaces that are dedicated but precisely spaces that are "left".

I think this is a beautiful challenge for urban planners, an invitation to renounce the dictates of design, from the author's point of view, to give space to other viewpoints, to other perspectives. Discovering that a space can be beautiful and functional even when it doesn't even seem planned. And to do so, the children's contribution will be important, perhaps indispensable. Whoever carries out the new city project will be a professional who will have learned to converse with children, to listen to them, to understand them, to work and to design with them. Anyone who knows how to take into account the children's point of view will find it natural to concern themselves with that of the elderly, of the disabled, of the poor.

The street, a place for everyone

"Street boy", "street woman" or the most recent "street children" are expressions that indicate reproach, condemnation, rejection. The street, a symbol of economic and moral degradation, is the place of maximum air pollution, of the uproar, of the danger arising from traffic; it is the place of robberies, of thefts, of the hawker; it is the place of the drugged, of the homeless, of the gypsies, of the beggars. Faced with this degradation, the city responds, as already said, defending itself. The street is an enemy and should be separated, isolated, abandoned. The decent citizen locks themselves in their home, is secured from the exterior and only travels through the street in the shelter of his car; if he has a dog, he uses the street as the place to take it to do its business. At the same time, people who are forced to live on the street see their conditions worsen and progressively move away from those who live locked in their homes.

On the one hand, the locked-up children, alone and entrusted to television; on the other, street children, who play in amongst filth, become out of control, aggressive and dangerous trying to obtain the necessities of life. Those confined in their home begin to fear the inhabitants of the street, avoid them, report them, even come to request their elimination, paying thugs, death squads. I am not outlining a possible plot of a science-fiction novel, but what is partly happening in many of our European cities and even in its terrifying but coherent culmination, the great South American metropolises.

Accepting the child as a parameter of change also, or perhaps primarily, means returning the social role, of a public place, of the encounter, of the walk and of the play that they have had, and that they must recover, to our streets. The streets will not become safe when they are guarded by the police, by the army or by voluntary patrols, but only when they are conquered by the children, the elderly, the citizens. The busy street will be clean again, will have sidewalks available to pedestrians, will again be beautiful, exciting to walk, to rest.

The more or less evident desire of the administrators, of the institutions, is to be able to bring back the lost, abandoned children from the street. For the most serious cases, one even thinks of imprisonment in jail or a special institution, but more commonly one thinks of school. The most widespread idea is that if they were able to take them to school, to the safe place of our children, they could recover. This is not true at all, unless the school is ready for a deep and radical conversion. In modern-day schooling, successful students patiently endure five hours of immobility, know how to read and write well, are willing to study even the most useless or, if anything, barely comprehensible things. These are the children who will always end up as the losers, who will end up defeated. When they no longer tolerate the humiliation of not understanding, of not passing, they will react, insurmountable conflicts will be born and they will return to the street.

Whether the school rejects them, or they reject the school does not change anything. The school will have failed and will be responsible for the major damage – returning those children to the streets humiliated and, therefore, in the best state to accept the "rescue" of anyone who believes in them by putting a drug dose or a gun in their hands.

So, an alternative solution seems more convincing and richer in possibilities – let us restore the street, free it from corruption, let the common and safe territory of these children, freer and more disadvantaged, be beautiful and healthy. Let it be enough to invite our children, those who are locked up at home, to come down and play with them, taking advantage of their ingenuity and skills. Maybe this way, all together, they would want to go somewhere, maybe even to school.[9]

The children that wait

Children often have to wait, sometimes a long time, while their parents wait in a line, wait for the train, visit a museum. Adults know how to wait, they know why they wait, they know how to spend time, or at least they know how to resign themselves to this necessity, but for children it is more difficult. For them, it makes no sense to stand still, in line, without doing anything. Then, they express their discomfort and become unbearable, they pitch a fit, thus making the situation of their parents and other adults even more difficult. Children are often considered bad, sometimes not very sensible, to their parents. The truth is that very often parents have no choice but to take their children with them and, when children are "bad," it means that they are living badly, that they are mistreated. The city should take care of this discomfort to the little ones by offering appropriate initiatives and structures. In public places, such as municipal offices and other administrations, in outpatient clinics, in museums, in railway stations, in airports, in all places, in short, where people wait and children have to wait with them, places should be opened where they can play together, find toys, read a book, draw, and so on. In some cases, a person will welcome them, help them have a good time, while the parents queue. With a little ingenuity, these different venues could organize games for children, relevant to their work, so that this idea would become a meaningful and original proposal. The post office, for example, could have a small room where children can play 'post office', with postmarks, scales, old stamps, writing letters, and so on.

These are initiatives that undoubtedly have their cost, but the discomfort of the citizens also has a cost. Today we have fewer children and therefore we have teachers to spare. Instead of inventing a thousand tricks to increase the number of teachers and reduce the number of students in each class, some of the former could, if they wish, assume these new roles of activity entertainers for children in the city. The proposal is not consistent with the complaint, several times highlighted, of separate and specialized places, but it seems a necessary minor evil in the hope of a city more suitable for children. This would mean small demonstrations of the city's affection for the smallest citizens, particularly appreciated by the adults.

---

[9] See file n.19: "A stone garden".

The mayor should tackle this problem first in the places of his competence such as the civil registry, municipal district boards, tax offices, to affirm in practice his position in favor of children, to educate by example. He could then invite all public and private entities to also think about the children and make the consultation and help of the Laboratory "The city of children" available.

Restaurant and hotel structures

Children are increasingly accompanying their parents to restaurants and hotels. They should be new, exciting, desirable experiences for them, just as they are in general for adults; instead, they are often overwhelming and disappointing.

In particular, children endure adult's schedule and pace poorly. Adults take a snack and talk, after eating they drink coffee and talk; children wait. Adults like to spend a lot of time sitting at the table, because it is a good opportunity to be together, to exchange opinions and information. The child is usually alone, also excluded from these conversations, which deal with topics that it does not know or is not interested in, such as secrets about different acquaintances or discussions about political matters. With the child, adults solve the problem of their presence and inclusion in the talk by asking them for some information about their school: it seems that the world of children begins and ends in the school classroom.

Then, there is the problem of the full plate and the adults' conviction that a child is not able to assess neither the quality nor quantity of food. For adults, eating is a pleasure, for children a duty. Naturally, this tends to create a rejection by children and therefore the daily conflict between what they want and what feels good.

Finally, the problem of freedom arises with the hotel. This special place, where there is someone who cleans, who makes the beds and where the elderly feel especially free, for children it is usually a place of many difficulties and limitations.

Children are aware of all this and have clear ideas when formulating proposals, as can be seen in Fano's experience.[10] They are simple, realizable proposals, that we, adults, might have thought as well. Children ask to eat together, serve themselves on their own, have more autonomy, manage their time. They ask for themselves, in short, what adults want for themselves.

---

[10] See the experience that is being developed in Fano mentioned in the file n.14: "A seal of quality for children in hotels and restaurants".

The pediatric hospital

The hospital should also be made suitable for the child, recognizing its rights, its characteristics, its needs; never forgetting that before being a patient he is a child.

The child should never go to the hospital if it is not absolutely essential; it should be the hospital that goes to the child, with its doctors, with its nurses, if necessary, with mobile units. A similar operation of the hospital should be more economical and less traumatic for small patients; it could avoid separating them from their homes, from their affections, from their securities.

When it is necessary for the child to go to hospital it is important that it does not sleep there. The moment of sleep is the one that creates the most emotionally upsetting experiences for the child. Similarly, at home, it is disregarded and for that reason, the complex rituals of accompaniment, of the story, of the goodnight kiss are created.

If the child must sleep in the hospital, there must be two beds, one for the child and one for any of its parents, in a cozy environment where it can be surrounded by its toys, the things to which it is emotionally linked. This, which today might seem like a luxury, should be possible in a hospital where you enter only in exceptional cases.

The admitted child should be in bed as little as possible if this is allowed by its physical condition. It is necessary to break that strange hospital habit that identifies the patient with their bed, which deprives them of all the symbols of their identity, even their clothes, preventing them from leaving, making them feel in a trap.

Naturally, if the young patient can be out of bed, it must have diverse places to spend time, in a pleasant and productive way, together with the other children admitted and with the friends who are going to visit him. Places to play, materials to play with, to paint, to manipulate, to build. These places can be enclosed or outdoors. It is appropriate that there is a cozier place to read, study, write, draw, provided with a good library, computer, various materials. A place to watch television, preferably closed-circuit TV, and with a good video library, to exclude the connections with TV shows that would make the child a slave of low-quality cartoons and advertising.

Naturally, these resources will also be available to children who cannot leave the bed, with adequate support (bedside tables, television in the rooms, mobile library). Appropriate solutions should also be studied when children are in particular physical (for example, when they cannot use a hand because they are being given I.V.) or psychological states (for example, when they lose their hair from chemotherapy). Special care must be taken when preparing children for the most traumatic situations, from injections to surgical intervention. That is why it may be important that there are corners where children can play doctors, using anesthesia masks, syringes, bandages, and so on. It's great that some hospitals call clowns to keep the small patients company. Even in this case, a good "doctor" clown (and in general they are good) can do a lot to eliminate children's fear.

Attending to its state of health, the child must be guaranteed its maximum connection with the outside world and especially with its friends, both for playing and for school. Care must be taken not to consider the school as the child's only interest and as the only link to the outside world. It would be good if friends could go at any time they want, without excessive limitations. If it coincides with that of the doctor's visit or that of simple medications it will prove to be a useful experience for them and may, with their presence, encourage the small patients.

The hospitalized child should not change its usual schedules. It is not easy to understand why a person who is sick, who must leave their usual place, who must prepare themselves for disturbing and often painful experiences, also has to radically modify their habits: to be woken up at dawn to measure their temperature, to eat at noon and have dinner at six o'clock, to face after that some very long days without knowing how to spend their time. The explanation that is always given to me is that these schedules are based on the auxiliary staff's shifts. But are we crazy? Is it possible that such a delicate service is subject to the conditions of those who provide it and not of who receives it? Habits, therefore, must be respected and so, for example, waking up for breakfast will be at eight o'clock, lunch at one o'clock in the afternoon and dinner at eight o'clock. Taking these schedules into account, the staff will decide freely and autonomously how to organize the shifts.

They should carefully avoid alarming images and suggestions, stark white walls, "hospital" stretchers, white uniforms, surgical instruments in sight and clinking on the cart, if only to change a bandage or take their temperature.

It would be good to listen to and consult children who must spend long periods of time in the hospital. There could be a Council of children that expresses their opinions, discusses with the doctors, prepares their messages, their manifests, in reserved spaces. An adult should follow this experience of participation to ensure its continuity. It could be a doctor or a nurse who wants, and is able to, expand their area of influence. Little things that, nevertheless, would make the little patients feel less strange and more involved.

The pediatric team must select and then train their collaborators, doctors and assistants, even for their ability to be around children. The City Council of Reggio Emilia, for example, has hired a puppeteer for its nursery school. A pediatric hospital could rightly have an entertainer, a clown, and so on. Some of these figures can certainly be among the staff on duty; others could be obtained through specific agreements with the Ministry of Education and the City Council.

In this case too, I think it is easy to understand the "instrumental" use of children. If the pediatric hospital were to be changed, the same could be done with the adult hospital too, because everything that has been said before for children, I believe, may also be valid for the elderly too.

I do not write these notes about the hospital only because of a consistent application of the general principles of the project, but because I have lived with a seven-year-old boy during the last five months of his life. This child was for me a great teacher. He had a brain tumor, he was calm, eager to play. He spent five months in bed, much of the time without actually needing it, to the point that some of his companions of misadventure did their therapy in hospital during the day. Most of the time he had an immobilized arm because he had an I.V. His mother spent five months in a chair, being able to open out a deck chair at night thanks to the tolerance of the staff. Although he was taken care of with all the necessary attention and even with much affection by all the staff, this child spent the last five months of his life without anyone, except his mother and his friends, worrying about his need to play. I shared this experience, so tough and so intense, like a great injustice. You cannot deprive a child of the possibility of playing. It cannot spend its last months like this.

A school suitable for children

I have worked as a researcher with the school and in the school for thirty years. I have actively participated in several proposals for methodological and pedagogical renewal and continue to deal with school and extracurricular education. But until I took care of the city; until it seemed absurd to me that the children had no voice or power in it as citizens; until we began to practice concrete forms of the children's participation in the reform and planning of the city (from the Children's Council to the project-executing children), until then I had not realized that, in school, children do not count for anything. Nobody cares to know their opinion. The school boards recognize student representation only in secondary schools. It is as if the children of three, of eight, of twelve years old, have no ideas, opinions, preferences.

On the other hand, no one is impressed, neither the teachers nor the parents, much less the children themselves, that the students do not like their school, that they attend reluctantly, that they want the arrival of recess, of Sunday, of vacation.

In the case of the city, we begin to think that it is not possible to do without the contribution of the children, even if the city is not made just for them. In the case of school, we continue to ignore them despite the fact that it is made only and specifically for them. In the case of the city, we have created a Children's Council,[11] asking each city school to send two representatives; but the schools of the city have not yet thought of giving themselves, at their core and for their functioning, a democratic organization.

A democratic experience

The school at all levels devotes some time to civic education. With this, it intends to teach the bases of democracy; but democracy cannot be taught, it must be lived. This could be an important first commitment that the school assumes by adopting the philosophy of this project – creating opportunities for real democratic participation in its management by students at each level.

This proposal could be made by giving maximum value to the class assembly, which could elect two representatives, a boy and a girl, to form the student council.[12] Representatives could meet periodically to discuss school problems and the proposals to be made. They could meet alone or with a delegated teacher that follows the tasks of the council. The school principal may request the Council's call to discuss some points of the school organization with the students' representatives.

From time to time, this Council, formed by students could meet with the faculty staff to transmit their proposals and protests, exactly as the Children's Council of Fano does, which is invited by the City Council to participate in the municipal plenary sessions and, as will happen soon, in the other municipalities that have been interested in the project.

It would be desirable that the School Student Council have financial resources, perhaps raised using the initiative of the students themselves, and also had a space to hold meetings, readily equipped: a mural space, open, reserved for the communication with school classmates.

---

[11] See file n.2: "The Children's Council".

[12] In Spain, there is a nationwide State School Council. In each Autonomous Community there is a School Council for its territorial scope, whose composition and functions will be regulated by a law of the Assembly of each Autonomous Community. The School Councils of the territorial areas are constituted by the director of the center and the representatives of the teachers, parents, students and administration and services staff.

It could have many operating hours according to its own recommendations. High-school students have been sending accurate data with their self-management experiences for a few years. It would be different if all students, from the first years of schooling, had their own spaces and time to express themselves, to protest, but also to propose and organize.

Naturally, this does not mean affirming that the school should be organized as the students want – it means that it makes no sense to think, manage, organize the school, disregarding what the students think. It means taking them into account. But it also means carrying out an experience of democracy, sometimes direct, sometimes delegated, which can certainly be worth much more than many civic education lessons.

When the city organizes its own Laboratory "The city of children" and creates a Children's Council, then each Student Council may choose two delegates, always a boy and a girl, to represent its institution. Delegates will not feel alone; they will have the possibility of transmitting, through the School Board and the class assemblies, the results of the meetings of the Children's Council to all the classmates and collect their proposals for the next meeting.

An experience of environmental education: Designing our own city

Nowadays, there is a lot of talk about environmental education and the school often engages in projects of this type, but almost always involving issues related to Nature or the problem of urban solid waste.

Forests, rivers, pollution, recycling or selective waste collection are studied. The first concern of environmental education should instead be to help students understand and control the environment they live in.

Knowing the environment by experiencing it, going through it, living it and then studying it effectively to understand its history, its characteristics, its limits, its resources, in anticipation of an active, real intervention, in collaboration or in conflict with the administrators, to guarantee the city itself a better future, a sustained development.

The school would thus become a laboratory for environmental studies and territorial intervention through the analysis of problems, making shared projects of urban spaces and seeking solutions to the identified problems. To do so, it will seek the collaboration of public offices (from the Property Registry to public works, from the municipal police to the Department of

Urban Planning) and from experts in the investigated sectors (architects, urban planners, sociologists, economists, etc.).[13]

The school could thus become an institution capable of committing itself, of carrying its action outside its walls, facing reality, with people, with the authorities, taking a position, protesting. In short, the school could write on its door those, so compromising, words that Don Milani wrote on the door of his school, in the parish of Barbiana: "I care".[14]

A road education experience: touring the city

The school develops road safety education programs and the City Councils make various materials available to the schools: videos, brochures, posters, and often also the local police; who attend classes to address this issue. These materials have a high cost and the obtained results are poor most of the time. In many cases, they are limited to lessons in road safety, presentation of traffic signs and the rules of the Highway Code. This is still the school that our children reject and thus, does not influence them. If the teacher is replaced by the police, the result does not improve, as this officer is also trying to teach a class and is not capable of doing so. In other words, we remove important professionals from our squares, from the streets, and have them do things they don't know how to do. The ideas that are communicated do not modify the real behavior at all, and are no use in shaping a more independent citizen who is aware of their rights and their duties.

On the other hand, the school, together with the families, could make it possible for the children to travel to school alone on foot by working with older students; allowing them to rediscover a little autonomy and test their rights and duties as pedestrians practically. This new experience can be discussed; initiatives can be channeled. Also, inspections can be carried out to check the different routes, to identify the most dangerous paths and study together the best way to avoid them. In this case, the police can be very useful by encouraging children and teachers to share their experience and knowledge of the Highway Code.[15]

---

[13] On these topics, see files n.11: "My city and I" and n.4: "The project-executing children".

[14] From English. It is the opposite of "I don't care" that is the translation of the fascist *Me ne fregó* ("I don't give a damn"). The inscription is still visible in Barbiana, at the door of the school.

[15] See files n.9: "Let's go to school alone" and n.10: "A pedestrian, cyclist and motorcyclist card".

The project "The city of children" is intended for the city and not for the school. This is not the ideal place for its development, but it is undoubtedly a very important place for children, who spend much of their childhood, adolescence and youth there. The school, therefore, can do a lot to assert this idea. It can help families understand and appreciate the value of the proposal. Furthermore, it can receive a lot by making the project their own philosophy, upholding its initiatives, participating in its activities, and mainly by recognizing the students' role of the protagonist; becoming, essentially, a children's school.

The neighborhood association: the right to play

The regulations of most neighborhood associations are illegal, illegitimate, as they violate a State law: The Convention on the Rights of the Child, approved by the United Nations in 1989[16] and adopted by the Spanish State in 1990.[17] Especially, Article 31 which approves the children's right to play. In the regulations of neighboring associations, obstacles to this right are often put down; sometimes it is not uncommon that its practice be totally prevented.

It is almost always forbidden to play on the stairs, in the hallways and even in the courtyards at certain times of the day, generally after eating, when adults are supposed to want a rest. I have not found an article in the text of the rights of man that defends adults' right to nap, whereas the one that defends the children right to play is very clear. Then again, the stairs have always been a good place to play, because of its articulated structure that allows hiding, chasing, but also sitting and chatting or arranging toys. However, with elevators today, they are practically no longer useful for developing games.

It is justly objected that children make noise, disturb. But doesn't the urban traffic, the excessive use of horns, and the already widespread use of the alarms disturb as well? No one has ever asked to prohibit the use of horns, alarms and for the suppression of traffic between two and four in the afternoon. So, what is happening to us adults? Are we becoming used to the terrible noise of alarms, the unpleasantness of the horns and the exasperating urban traffic and no longer know how to withstand the, no doubt annoying,

---

[16] The United Kingdom ratified the Convention on 16 December 1991, with several declarations and reservations, and made its first report to the Committee on the Rights of the Child in January 1995. The United States government played an active role in the drafting of the Convention and signed it on 16 February 1995, but has not ratified it.

[17] See the text of the Convention reproduced in Appendix 1.

but healthy and necessary, racket of the children who play? What society are we preparing for our children, for our grandchildren?[18]

In the current situation of environmental danger, which makes even the smallest freedom of children difficult, the community playground could and should be the optimal place for the autonomous play of children, even for the very young ones.[19] However, we adults have considered it more comfortable to prohibit this space for children's play (in addition to the other time prohibitions, it is almost always forbidden to play with a ball), instead allocating it to the parking of our cars. In this way, a common space, and therefore public, has been privatized, its use has been restricted, it has become ugly and dirty (also the cleanliness of the cars leaves much to be desired).

The mayors are the representatives of the citizens and should be so in a special capacity for the younger citizens. It would be fair, then, to invite the neighborhood associations to review their statutes making them respectful of the laws of the State and therefore of the rights of children. Also, they should rethink the use of community yards and notify the mayor or the Laboratory of any remodeling or restructuring. It would be necessary for neighborhood associations to discuss the modification of their statutes and primarily social use of their courtyards. These can become a meeting place, of socialization and recreation for children, for the elderly, for all neighbors. To do this, they will have to be restructured and equipped properly, solving private parking problems another way. If it is easier for children to leave home and go alone to the playground, adults will also be calmer and freer.

This invitation from the mayor, with adequate support from the local press, could be a major opportunity to open a debate in the city about children, about their complicated status as citizens, about their needs, about their rights.

Children's right to vote

Some time ago, a journalist asked me for my opinion on the reduction of the proposed voting age in Germany. I replied that I would have preferred that all citizens have the right to vote from birth, so that everyone counts in the taking and influencing decisions. This means that in a family made up of parents and

---

[18] The head of the local police in Turin said that twenty years ago he received many claims and requests for intervention daily for the inconvenience caused by children. Today he no longer receives them.

[19] See the experience of Manfred Drum, who made a network of spaces for pedestrian mobility and play in Munich by connecting several community courtyards, in the context of participatory projection work (Drum, 1995).

three children, five people could vote. Naturally, until the child has reached the legal age, it will be his legal guardians who exercise the right to vote. The first objection that could be made to this proposal is that voting is not a joke, that it is not delegated to anyone, that the parents would use the children's vote to favor their own parties. Again, the gruesome image of the adult "childeater": the driver of a car that can't wait to run over the child who crosses the street, the passerby who will almost certainly use violence on an unaccompanied child, the father who steals his son's vote. But the adults are us, we are the ones who drive the cars, the ones that run into the children who are alone in the street, who would use their vote. Moreover, we do not take into account that parents already choose for their children in matters much more delicate and important than what an electoral vote may be, and could not avoid doing so. They choose whether or not to baptize the child – whatever the decision, it strongly commits and shapes the child. They decide when and to which school to send it to, they guide their future choices. They decide to what extent they grant autonomy, with the consequences that derive from this, which have been spoken about in the first part of this book. They give children a cultural, ideological, political, moral reference, which is often very clear; trusting that they will not betray these ideals.

A second objection that could be made is that there is a risk of triggering more or less explicit propaganda campaigns to condition children, so that they in turn condition their parents' political choices. But isn't this exactly what happens every day, at all times, especially in children's television programs, with the advertising of countless products? But it is clear that in an ideological but deeply consumerist society like ours, everything that is linked with consumption seems normal and almost essential – yet one cannot joke about politics!

A proposal such as this, which may only seem provocative and whose difficulties of application are evident, does not pose a constitutional incompatibility with the Italian law[20] and it seems to me that it contains some interesting positive aspects.

The child, currently irrelevant, almost invisible in our society, would acquire influence and relevance.

Parents, also having to vote on behalf of their children, could raise the question of to what extent their parties are interested in the problems and needs of the children. On the other hand, the parties would quickly concern

---

[20] It would be interesting, however, if a mayor found a way for the children of his city to express themselves also with some form of a vote.

themselves with including these almost ignored problems in their programs to gain parental support.

Finally, as the children grow, they would begin to ask their parents how they intend to use their vote, they would like to understand or discuss the decisions. It seems to me that it would be a good way to talk about politics within our homes, instead of betting on one or another of the politicians of the political scene in spite of the total disinterest of young people. Perhaps they would hate politics less, help us understand it better, and help politicians practice it more credibly.

Chapter 7

Rethinking the city

Rethinking the city, loving it differently, making it suitable for everyone, including children, is an urgent need; not going back, not waiting for a return to the romantic climate of the town or the neighborhood forty or fifty years ago, but preparing it for a different future, which is not under the exclusive control of commercial production, which is not dominated by cars or the unstoppable development of services.

It's about thinking of a more agile, simpler city, in which all citizens count more.

The city of the present is a city that is left disrupted by cars, by their noise, by their fumes, by their vibrations. A city that falls helplessly into the hands of delinquency and organized crime, which have transformed the public land into scorched earth, making it unworkable for honest citizens. They are locked in their home, they move by car, they dream of the city transmitted through cables, of virtual offices. It will no longer be necessary to leave, move, we can work from our homes, using our computers in telematic networks. Some, who present themselves as experts, say that the traffic problem will then be solved, instead we will cram the information highways. In this case, however, we will have to face new problems that computer specialists have not considered, such as the irritating coexistence of family members, the definitive physical separation with respect to others and the city.

I am using the computer, email, Internet, as important and exciting tools for work and communication, but I would like to continue meeting up with friends and move more and better in a city that knows how to be beautiful.

If the city were a natural ecosystem, it would die in a very short time –its complexity has transformed into the simplified reality of separation and specialization. It has accepted that its citizens have become increasingly passive by offering continuous solutions, benefits, assistance in the form of services. Its balance, its survival depend less and less on its resources and more and more on external factors that it does not control and cannot guarantee.

Rethinking the city means having a project for the future, preparing, as environmentalists say, sustainable development. A controlled, not selfish, development that finds enough strength and energy in itself to guarantee its future and that of the next generations. The child is the natural guarantee of sustainable development – it must become older, be capable of solving problems, and he will never be able to do so if we do not ensure its autonomy, the possibility of risk and growth, the possibility of fun and spontaneous relationships. Similarly, citizens must regain their ability to solve problems through agreement, solidarity, collaboration, without waiting for the intervention of the relevant authorities.

Rethinking the city means preparing a future in which there is a desire and opportunity to think about well-being and the quality of life. A future in which young people still feel the thrill, the emotion, the desire to bring children into the world.

In rethinking the city, however, we must be conscious that the child is not confined to a kind of "Indian reservation", where everything is permitted or ideal, but clearly separated from the real world, that of the adults. In this "reservation", children could be granted the opportunity to express themselves, express their needs, also practice forms of democracy, present projects to be carried out. But a Children's Council, a garden or a monument designed by the children does not mean that the city is open to debate and wants to change. The risk is that outside the "reservation" the city will behave the same as always, and that once the children are pleased the adults, acquitted of their feelings of guilt, can say: "Where were we?", and continue with their serious speeches of politics and economics.

That is why I feel the need to confirm once again, at the risk of being repetitive, that "The city of children" is not a project for children, but for the city.

And what the child can represent for the city, the cities can represent for our country: politics, good administration, participation and democratic control begin with the cities; as well as the welcome, the solidarity. In a time of such widespread and serious social and moral degradation, children will be able to save our cities and consequently our country. I am often told that this is a utopia, madness, and I agree. But it is much more utopian and crazier to proceed along the path of no future which our cities have followed.

The city of children is a concrete utopia, a sustainable utopia.

A difficult project to carry out, like all utopias. For this purpose, I remember the quotation of a lady from Viareggio that moved me a lot. At the end of my presentation of the project, a man had asked for the floor, saying that he liked it very much, considered it fair and desirable but that, according to him, it would never come to fruition when taking into account the administrative slowness, bureaucratic obstacles, the interests called into question. The lady replied: "I do not know if it can ever be done, but I am sure that we, in any case, are already winning."

In short, the lady said that if we manage to include the child in our political debate, if we manage to discuss the children with the mayors, with the local police, with the economists, with the engineers of the Town Halls, with the doctors of the hospital, with restaurateurs, with teachers and with parents, we are already winning! It is undoubtedly a minimal result, but it is a way to start building the future.

Allow me a reflection at the end of these pages. Writing this book, carrying out some evaluation, I realized that I started working on the project "The city of children" after becoming a grandfather. I don't think this is a coincidence. Parents are young, eager to perform in life, they need affirmation and therefore end up accepting many commitments. I don't think of moral commitments, but of agreements with the administration, those I was talking about at the beginning of the book: services, help, assistance to support a hostile city, because this is the shortest, safest way, and when we are young there is no time to lose, you cannot risk too much. Then, the search for a place in a nursery, perhaps changing the place of residence,[1] the search for the nursery school with the most extended schedule, the full day, are requirements that cannot take into account the child's own needs. Parents are in a hurry; they look for the most "functional" solutions. The grandparents, on the other hand, have the time of those who no longer have a career to build or ambitions to achieve. And so, they can afford to become radical in their decisions, no longer accept commitments and seek new perspectives, a possible future for their grandchildren and for the children to come.

---

[1] There are even girls who do not marry to have more points, such as single mothers, to secure a place for their child in the nursery.

Third part:
The experiences

Chapter 8

The files

This third part presents activities, initiatives, projects, that emerge, to a great extent, from the experience of the Fano Laboratory. These should neither be considered an organic proposal nor a forced, or even suggested, path – they are intended to be a modest, but optimistic, testimony of the possibilities of the project's realization that we have presented in the first part of this book.

It is often said that in Fano it is too easy, but that it will be difficult to propose the same in the big cities. I think there is something true and something false in both statements. It is true that radical experiences like these are more easily developed in small or medium-sized cities. I think about the experience of the local services for children of Reggio Emilia or Pistoia, the educational experience of Mario Lodi in Piadena; I think, obviously, of Don Milani's experience in Barbiana. Undoubtedly, the small city is healthier, it has been able to defend its identity and social relations better, participation and solidarity are easier for it. But it is completely wrong to think that this facilitates the fulfilment of a project like this. The small city already participates, thanks to the globalizing effect of television, in all the social and cultural phenomena of the country, sharing the worst experiences with the big cities, from drugs to racism, from fear of separation, from the power of the parties to the request of assistance by the local entity. This makes every proposal for change, especially if it is radical, meets a firm resistance. Fano's experience was always and is still conflictive. I always protested before the three mayors who succeeded one another since the opening of the Laboratory, for their indifferent support of our proposals, for their lack of courage to dare more. But this has never made me forget that the administrators of Fano wanted and defended the Laboratory "The city of children", despite knowing that it would be a thorn in their side.

I am also convinced that no city is too large or devastated that it has lost all desire and inclination to think about its future with hope and willingness to change. This is what the responses of cities like Rome and Palermo tell me, or like Rosario, in Argentina, which certainly cannot be considered small and easy realities, and where this project is finding the first forms of receptivity and fulfillment.

1. Fano, "The city of children"

A municipal Laboratory for the study, projection and experimentation of changes in the city adopting the child as a parameter

The City of Fano, already devoted to the development of a policy of services for children, opened in 1991 a Laboratory called "The City of Children"[1] which, on the one hand, wants to be a point of reference for citizens, the associations, the children; and on the other, an incentive for the mayor, the councilors, the specialists, so that they do not forget the commitment made to adopt the child as a parameter in the development of the city.

Logo of the Laboratory "The City of Children" of Fano.

The Laboratory is a bet, a challenge. A city that has grown according to the demands, the requirements of the adults, that chooses to change its outlook and is therefore exposed to a continuous contradiction.

---

[1] For contact or material orders: Laboratory *La città dei bambini*, Corso Matteotti, 66, 61032 Fano (Italy), tel. 07 39 721887374, fax 803273. For national coordination see file n.24: "A national network that goes beyond".

Fano is not the city of children. It is, however, a city that has accepted this challenge and imposed an internal structure that condemns the contradiction and proposes the change.

To give credit where it's due, Fano has also done something that is increasingly evident and must be mentioned – it has included the laboratory in its organic plan as an organizational unit, with its own headquarters equipped with modern computer facilities, with full-time staff dedicated to their activities; it has asked this writer to take over its scientific direction. A specialized committee, formed by the representatives of the different councils, has just been set up to closely monitor the activities of the Laboratory and ensure its overall vision. The presentation before the Laboratory is currently assigned to the councilor for Educational Policy. In addition, Fano's City Council has recognized and sustained the various initiatives that the Laboratory has launched in these years and that will be presented in the files. In other aspects, however, the City Council is unable to adjust itself to the pace of the Laboratory and the children. It is delayed with respect to the promised accomplishments, it is not always consistent in the initiatives, it usually resists stimuli. In short, it is a relationship of great interest, in which the conflict reveals both support and difficulties.

The Laboratory has been recognized by the Italian Ministry of the Environment as a territorial laboratory for environmental education[2] and as such has been funded under the Triennial Environmental Program.

From the beginning, Fano has set itself objectives of activities in the city itself, and broader objectives with regard to the promotion of the project in other Italian municipalities.

It is related to national and international movements and associations such as "Educating cities", UNICEF, European Union, ANCI,[3] Arciragazzi, CGD, The Possible City, Ligambiente, INU, WWF.

---

[2] In recent years, a national plan for environmental education is being carried out with the help of the Ministry of Environment and the one of Education, which have signed a program agreement. The national plan foresees the opening of Territorial Laboratories, as a regulation outside of school, open to the meeting, exchange and support of all those who, from any sector, are interested in environmental education. It is also part of the premises of this project that environmental education is not considered only or especially a concern for nature, but is concerned with a recovery of the citizen's relations with their environment, with a view to sustainable development. Therefore, the Fano Laboratory is considered with all authority of environmental education.

2. The Children's council

The guarantee of the children's point of view

In Fano's experience, from the first year on, it was thought that children should be the protagonists of the project and that, therefore, they should be given adequate opportunities to express themselves and make suggestions. A Children's Council was created, considered as a need for a child presence in this small great revolution that was proposed to the administrators. At least until now, giving this Council the functions of a municipal Children's Council had not been thought of; with their parties, their electoral campaign, their young mayor, their councilors, etc. An idea that, on the other hand, has a long tradition in France and has also been present in Italy for a few years. It is certainly a useful and beautiful experience for children who participate in such initiatives, but often their participation is limited to developing their own projects and following them until they are completed, asking adults for new possibilities and openings, but not necessarily modifying its city government project. In the case of Fano, however, the objective is, as it has been repeated several times, exactly this – change the city, change the culture of the adults based on the child's perspective. The purpose of the Children's Council is, therefore, that of the Laboratory's advisory body, which guarantees officials the point of view of children, not only on issues of strictly child interest, but also on all issues of the city that the Laboratory faces.

Structure and operation

The Council is made up of one boy and one girl, for each of the primary schools, for a total of about thirty counselors. So far, there have been no precise rules for the election of counselors and each school behaves differently: voluntary candidacy by children, direct election and perhaps other systems.

Children are elected for a period of two years and it is suggested that they begin their term in fourth grade of elementary school and finish in fifth grade (eight to ten years old). Made up of one counselor of fourth grade and one of fifth grade for each school, the Council renews half of its members every year, ensuring continuity in the operation and transfer of competencies of outgoing children to incoming students. The biennium seems necessary to us so that

---

[3] ANCI: Associazione Nazionale Comuni Italiani (The National Association of Italian Municipalities); CGD: Coordinator Genitori Democratici (Democratic Parenting Coordinator); INU: Istituto Nazionale di Urbanistica (Italian National Institute of Urban Planning); WWF: World Wildlife Fund.

children can assume the role of representatives and perform it consciously. Representation is learned and, in general, the youngest children or those at the beginning of the mandate intervene above all to communicate their personal ideas; they hardly feel "representative" of their peers; they rarely take notes to inform correctly or ask teachers for more time and possibilities to communicate with other students in the class or with those in other classes. We respect this gradual process, without excessive demands. In a few months, the young counselors assume their role and end up defending it firmly, strong enough and convinced enough to get angry with the teachers who do not grant them the necessary time, sometimes question my direction of the Council, write letters to the mayor or the newspapers, even adopt positions that do not match our own. I remember, as an example, what a child counselor once said: "The teacher does not let us do the assembly to discuss with classmates and prepare the Council because she says there is no time. But then we ended up talking about civic education!"

It was suggested to start with the fourth year because the children already have good control of their communication mechanisms and because they can conclude the mandate with the end of elementary school. In general, children live this experience with great interest and participation, it is rare for someone to leave before finishing their term and often the former counselors ask us to continue with some similar initiative.[4]

The Council meets once a month at the headquarters of the Laboratory, is chaired by the scientific director, and the discussions are recorded in the minutes. Children are usually accompanied by their parents, but adults cannot participate except in special cases. In addition to the members of the Laboratory, administrators or occasional visitors who have requested may attend the Council, but this occurs rarely and they usually attend as listeners.

The Council is convened by means of a personal letter containing the agenda. It faces the different problems that the Laboratory is dealing with, such as traffic, pediatric hospitals, playgrounds, the relationship with the elderly, children going to school unaccompanied, restructuring of restaurants and hotels, or topics proposed by the children themselves.

When there are several issues that must be submitted to the Council's analysis, working groups are formed that are also convened with on a biweekly basis.

---

[4] See file n.16: "The COC Club".

Once a year, the members of the Children's Council participate in an extraordinary session of the Municipal Council, with the right to speak, representing all the children of Fano.

3. The Municipal council, open to children

Since 1991 the mayor of Fano has joined the initiative of the Italian UNICEF, "The mayor, defender of childhood", which plans to dedicate an extraordinary session of the Municipal Council to children annually. After the first experience in 1991, when a session was devoted to childhood problems, with invited experts, it was decided to open the Council to children and give them the floor. Over a few weeks the children of the Council discuss, in their respective schools, problems they encounter in the city, things that do not work, and prepare proposals. These are discussed in a plenary session of the Children's Council and some of the young counselors present them in the Municipal Council. It is preferred that no more than seven or eight report, so that they can adequately explain the points under discussion and answer any adult questions. The session is also attended by children from other courses, until completing the public gallery of the municipal council room.

The proposals

The following are some of the proposals that children have presented during these years and that the Council has somehow collected:

When you decide something about the city there should also be someone who knows the children (1992).

The Board agreed that all of the city's modification projects should be sent to the Laboratory, which would be able to express an opinion that reflected the views of the children.

Cars take up too much space in the streets and take it away from the game (1993).

The Councilor for Traffic promised to close the whole city to cars for a whole day per year, so that the children could play in the streets. This tradition has been repeated for three years.[5]

---

[5] See file n.13: "A day without cars."

One day a policeman took my ball because I was playing in the square.
If someone wants to play in a sports field they must be a member and, if
not, they must pay admission.
We want to go to school alone, but the cars do not respect the zebra
crossings and are parked on the sidewalks, so we must walk in the road
(1996).

The Municipal Council approved an agenda to discuss and vote on three issues: the first, on the right of children to play as they wish in all city squares; the second, to review the contracts for the transfer of the areas to the sports associations to guarantee a free time slot of the facilities; and the third, on the rigorous application of the rules that defend and protect pedestrians and especially children – the priority of zebra crossings and the protection of sidewalk space. It was requested that each of the raised issues should have adequate publicity, in order to help raise public awareness.

The adults

For the first Council open to children, when the Children's Council did not yet exist, no particular instructions had been given and the students had prepared their requirements in their respective schools. To our great surprise, the children talked only about their classes and their schools: the danger, the noise, the absence of curtains, the lack of maintenance and cleaning. We were amazed at the children's interest in their school, but then it became clear that it was the teachers who had suggested the protests and the proposals.

Since then, a letter sent to the schools warns that the proposals of the children must abide by the child's relationship with the city, its autonomy, its possibilities of playing, and not the school which, if deemed necessary, will find other occasions to express its needs. The preparation of the Municipal Council takes place in the Children's Council, where proposals arising from the debates held in their classes are collated and coordinated.

If it is not easy for teachers to respect the freedom of students, it is not easy for administrators to find appropriate behavior in response to the children's requirements. A temptation, evident in the first editions of the Open Council, was to use the meeting to scold the children. These protested, for example, the dirt in the gardens, and the administrators replied by advising the children to be the first not to throw paper and cans around. Another temptation, still present in part, is the defense, of always saying that things are already being done, without trying to understand exactly what those strange and different citizens are asking. One more sign of the discomfort of adults is their difficulty in talking with children, asking them to explain themselves better, to go deeper into detail. This difficulty conceals the distrust of the children's true capacity, always considering them as smaller than they really are.

It must be said, in defense of adults, that it is not easy to understand children; it takes good intentions, curiosity, but also preparation, which derives from study and experience.

An example:
In one of the first municipal councils open to children, one of them, who lived in an urbanization, said: "I would like to go to the city by bicycle, but my mother is afraid." The easiest interpretation was that he was asking us for a bicycle lane, so we sent a crew to paint a yellow line that separates the bicycle lane from the car lane. The Councilor for Traffic showed good intentions, but did not give an answer to the child. The mother, in fact, continued to be afraid of possible reckless or drunk drivers who could have failed to respect the yellow line and forbade the use of the bicycle again. The attentive administrator, nonetheless, should have called a specialist and said: "Prepare a project for a bicycle road so that mothers can stop being afraid." Then, an insurmountable barrier could be proposed for cars or, better still, the use of secondary roads as a route for bicycles. If the children had been consulted, they would surely have known how to help the specialist.

Helping adults listen and understand children and know how to converse with them is perhaps the most important task of the Laboratory, even more so than the construction of sidewalks and the organization and implementation of the various initiatives.

4. The project-executing children

A new form of participatory architecture

Since 1992, an experience of planning spaces and urban equipment has been carried out in Fano in which children from kindergarten and primary school participate. The experience includes, as experts and presenters, young architects who work with children's groups. The first year, our specialists worked as collaborators of an experienced architect presenter;[6] since the second year the specialists from this sector have been responsible for the city of Fano and now they also offer their specialty to other cities interested in the project.

---

[6] On the activity of Raymond Lorenzo, the architect who has made this first experience in Fano, see file n.20: "Other experiences: the planning shared with children".

The method

The groups usually work on school premises, with schedules that coincide with the classes; but these conditions can be modified. For example, heterogeneous groups can be formed by age levels, work also in the afternoon, and even meet in places other than the schools. In our experience, we have observed that, when these changes are possible, participation is greater and the children are more motivated.

In the four years of activity, several issues have been proposed to children following the programming of the project "My city and me".[7] In any case, they are true, free spaces, in which a restructuring is legitimate and possible, although there are no guarantees that the projects will be accepted and carried out.

This creates a new condition in the relationship between students, school and city, because students are invited to intervene in real spaces with concrete proposals that will then be presented, not to the parents or the principal, but to the mayor and competent councilors. But, what is the objective? To make administrators aware of the views, demands and proposals of children so that a professional can take them into account when they hand over the spaces they have designed. If later this specialist is able to involve, even in the phase of execution and implementation planning, the children who have worked on the project, they will have made an important contribution to the training of new, interested and participative citizens.

The most delicate problem in this work is to get children to express themselves with their authentic creativity and imagination, without making them say what we want them to say. On one hand, therefore, children are helped to free themselves from stereotypes; on the other, their ideas are respected.

If we ask a group of children to tell us how they would like to equip their own playground, they are likely to respond by proposing the same stereotypes several times indicated on these pages: with slides, swings and merry-go-rounds.

There are several paths to allow children to express themselves more freely. One is the analysis of the games they prefer, the most attractive places for them and, from this, discover their characteristics and try to recreate them in the space to be designed. Another is the consideration of the proposals presented by other children in other cities and in other countries. It is, in any case, about children becoming aware that "you can go further", that there are no limits to imagination, even if then you have to face reality, with materials, with the laws of physics, with the costs.

---

[7] See file n.11: "My city and I".

After the phase of study and conception of ideas it is important to arrive at the realization of a project and, if possible, of a model. Children, boys, like to "see", to "touch" their ideas. Their model becomes their notebook, their book, with which they communicate and defend their ideas.

The children's proposals

After four years and a few projects, what can we observe in the children's proposals? We have engaged children in various topics such as squares and monuments, recovery of abandoned spaces, the relationship with cars.

In relation to playing, children manifest a clear opposition to traditional proposals: they like to hide, look for corners at ground level or climb on something; have water at their disposal, earth, grass, plants; be able to use different materials to do what they want to do at any moment. In their gardens there are, therefore, frequent slopes, caves, towers, cabins, forts, small lakes, ponds, fountains, canals; logs, stones, sand. It is as if they were telling us, in short: "Give us a rich, modular, non-trivial, unstructured space, and we will know how to use it."

Regarding the squares and monuments, there is a very clear rejection of the presence of cars in these "public" spaces – the squares must be returned to the citizens to meet, to sit down, to play. Children defend them with barriers, with walls, with water canals, and provide them with benches, kiosks, trees. They have suggested a proposal that is both interesting and very close to the most modern ideas: a monument that can be visited, that is available for use and for playing. In those same years, monuments appeared in Barcelona that are also great toys: for example, the one that represents a matchbox or the letters of the alphabet.

As for the street-car relationship and the children's desire to move on their own, their proposal is twofold: on the one hand, the routes must be protected; on the other, they must be interesting and beautiful. Children imagine paths reserved for pedestrians, separated from the street of cars by walls or stakes, sometimes even closed such as transparent plastic tunnels. The streets can be crossed by bridges or underground passages to avoid any dangerous encounters with the enemy – the car.

In relation to this first proposal, although it is an important complaint against the excessive power of cars, and is in agreement with what is gleaned from the projects, I do not agree with the children at all. As I have said several times, the purpose of the Laboratory is for the child to go down the street to save it. The child, with its presence, with the express display of his rights and those of all pedestrians, will force cars to be more respectful and less numerous, to retreat to more adequate and less invasive spaces. On the other hand, what the children propose is the path of separation and defense again, and it is seen as ineffective.[8] The example of pedestrian walkways or underground passages is valid for all, apparently the safest solutions to cross dangerous streets. In fact, these passages are not especially used by children because the subway is generally disturbing and smelly. The bridge, on the other hand, represents a long and tiring path. So, it is preferred to cross the street, and the situations of greatest danger are created: the driver who sees the walkway will drive calmly, thinking that whoever wants to cross will have to use it and, therefore, will not be alert in case some passer-by unexpectedly crosses the road. In these cases, a traffic light operated by pedestrians who want to cross is better. It is better not to separate, but to meet and live together, so that one and the other exercise mutual respect.

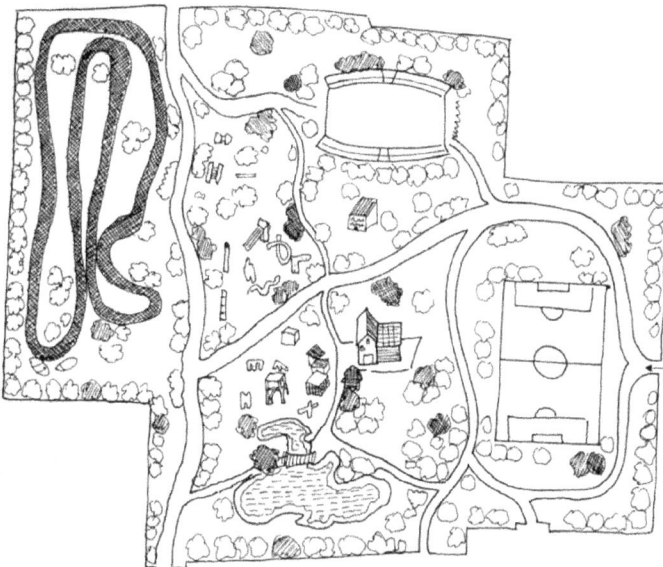

Project for children in fifth grade at the Montessori Elementary School in Fano.[9]

---

[8] Nor is it correct to think that this idea of fear, even extreme separation, corresponds to childish thinking. It is in contrast, for example, with the results of the surveys of the "Let's go to school alone" initiative, in which children are less fearful than their parents about the dangers of traffic. And in this case, it is actually a lived experience! (See file n.9: "Let's go to school alone").

[9] Presented in 1993 and approved by the municipal government and financed in 1995 for its realization. The architect, who is currently the face of the final project, has resumed contact with the teenagers who had taken care of the first project and they will thus be able to continue their implementation.

5. The little guides

A different way to know and love the city

Continuing with the objective of making children have an active and leading role in the life of the city, so that they are (and not "become") mindful citizens, we invite the adult and elderly citizens, who know and love the city of Fano, to give the children some of their time. We asked them to take a group of children "by the hand" and accompany them to observe and feel the city, so that they can meet it in a non-academic way but directly and 'in the flesh', so that they could then share their experience and explain it to their classmates. Each of these "street teachers" proposed a tour and lived an experience with their elementary and secondary school students that covered about ten itinerant meetings. A teacher or a member of the Laboratory was also part of each group. Some proposed the Roman city; others the Medieval and Renaissance; others the popular one of the alleys; others an urban interpretation.

One objective of the activity was to form little guides who were capable of accompanying the children who come to Fano every year in spring at the end of the "My city and I" campaign, and the adults that the Laboratory invites to the city for the different activities. The Agency for Tourism Promotion valued this initiative by inviting the little guides to accompany groups of adults visiting the city on several occasions. A true experience that the children took part in with great enthusiasm and self-confidence.

This is also a simple experience, which costs almost nothing and offers children the opportunity to get to know and love their own city.

The difficulty we encountered was the limited availability of adults, of well-informed retirees, to offer part of their time to the children. That is why we only managed to carry out this experience twice: Laboratory's task for the child to occupy a place in the minds of adults is still ongoing. We will have to make our fellow citizens understand that what we ask of them is not a pleasure, it is not a gift, but a duty. Those who have had the good fortune to know, to study, to love their city, have the duty to transmit this wealth to the children so that they know how to be curious, interested and affectionate citizens with respect for their city.

6. The reunion of the City commission government

The child in the mind of the adults

If the city wants to adopt the child as a parameter of change, if it wants to accept this revolutionary challenge, its administrators must put themselves in the attitude of those who do not know, and wants to enter, the unknown world of childhood. If this attitude is missing, adherence to the project is only apparent and instrumental.

In Fano's experience, a meeting of the City commission government is held every year in which the mayor, the councilors and the entire government team participate. The meeting, organized and coordinated by the Laboratory, plans moments of study and deepening the understanding of children's issues, and moments of programming activities for the next year. It is celebrated in a convent outside the city and lasts the whole day. This way the inconvenience of the phone is avoided and a sufficient period of useful work is ensured. Particularly in the early years, there was a fear of the politicians' and especially the municipal government team's reactions, who could have considered this initiative a waste of time. But this never happened, and the desire to repeat the meeting more frequently has always arisen.

During the year, the Laboratory is convened several times as it participates in regular sessions of the municipal plenary session and on many occasions proposes and obtains the holding of extraordinary meetings to face and solve organizational problems related to the various initiatives it promotes, meetings in which all councilors and those responsible for the municipal services concerned participate.

The need for so much contact with the Administration, in addition to the constant collaboration with the councilor delegated by the Laboratory, confirms the complexity and difficulty of the project. The regulations and, moreover, the administrative tradition, are not favorable to children. The current trend of adults is to protect children more than to favor their autonomy. That is why it takes a lot of good will and a little creativity to move between laws, notices and regulations that, without a doubt, are not intended for them.

7. "The local police, a friend of the children"

In the last two years, the Traffic Department organized an updating and training course for all the local police officers of the Fano City Council. Taught by the Laboratory "The city of children", it is entitled "The local police, a friend of the children". During the meetings, the current role of the local police was analyzed, a role essentially oriented towards traffic control and car parking. The agent, who sees his role degraded, does not like to be considered hostile by his fellow citizens. Therefore, we analyzed the possibility that the police could assume a guarantor role, in a new perspective of greater urban mobility by pedestrians and cyclists, starting with children. The proposal awakened interest, and new functions and new modalities of presence and intervention are being evaluated. For example, the "Let's go to school alone" initiative suggests that the police officer should no longer monitor and control the entry into schools that are freed from the siege and danger of the cars belonging to parents accompanying their children. They should instead be present in the neighborhood, walking the streets to encourage drivers to take into account the children's mobility rights, even punishing them if they do not respect the priority of zebra crossings or park on sidewalks reducing the autonomy of pedestrians. After the first year of the "Let's go to school alone" initiative, in one of the two neighborhoods involved, citizens have asked the neighborhood police to intervene to protect the autonomy of children. The Administration has taken into account this request and is currently in the experimentation phase.

In the next meetings, it will be necessary to continue the elaboration of this new function and of the new attitudes that the local police may adopt to favor the autonomy of the citizens; participating, in this way, as protagonists in the realization of the new city that is being designed.

8. The fine of the children

The children of the Council and, through them, all their schoolmates, can use a "moral" fine, which requires limited dimensions. Children know they must "fine", not to sanction any violation of the street code, because this is the task of the local police, but only when motorists' behavior generates obstacles that limit the freedom and autonomy of the pedestrians. It is especially used in cases where cars are parked on sidewalks, which presents children with the unnecessary risk of going down the road. The "fining" was carried out in collaboration with the Traffic Department and seemed to have some effectiveness. Children say that adults are embarrassed when they find this child reproach on the windshield of their car and do not usually commit the offense again.

Beyond effectiveness, it seems important to give children civil "weapons" with which to express their disagreement and claim their own rights. I believe that the use of the fine is worth more than many lessons on street education and its dangers.

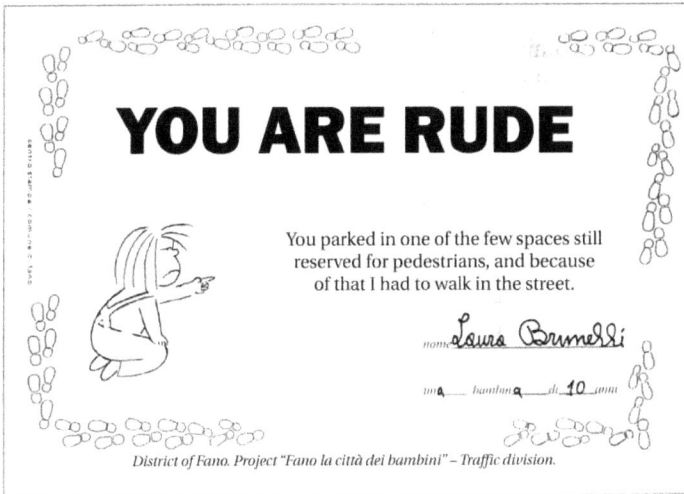

YOU ARE RUDE

You parked in one of the few spaces still
reserved for pedestrians, and because
of that I had to walk in the street.

Laura Brunelli

ina ___ bambina ___ di __10__ anni

District of Fano. Project "Fano la città dei bambini" – Traffic division.

A model of "moral" fine realized with the collaboration between the children of the Council and the Traffic Department of Fano.[10]

9. "Let's go to school alone"

First and small experience of autonomy

The Laboratory "Fano, the city of children" launched an experience called "Let's go to school alone" in the 1994-1995 school year. It's about allowing elementary-school children to go to school and go home unaccompanied, on foot. It is a small experience with respect to the general objective of giving children the possibility of leaving home alone, but it is a way of opening a gap in the already widespread and exaggerated protection of families and the social mistrust.

It is a possible experience because it provides a clear route for a limited time that is always the same, which allows the simultaneous participation of many children of different ages.

Even though Fano is a small city, it was preparing for several months before being able to address this proposal. The main problem is the distrust that parents have regarding other adults and their children. To help overcome their

---

[10] If someone wants to take advantage of this fine model for their children or their students to use, simply photocopy it, delete the name and age, increase it and make many copies. It is advisable that children color the large letters.

fear, it was necessary to limit the invasion and arrogance of the cars and mend a network of welcoming and social solidarity that would make this experience possible; including the different protagonists of neighborhood life.

The children

We believe that this initiative can have several positive effects: offering children a small chance of autonomy, facing the problems of travel and some risks that they can easily control on their own; suggesting behaviors of cooperation and solidarity beginning with the presence of the youngest, disabled, or isolated classmates; breaking the rigid experience among children of the same age that the school proposes. We knew that we could count on the interest and enthusiasm of the children, which was already proven in the Children's Council.

The teachers

This initiative was discussed with principals and teachers for a long time, certain that the school could do much to support and value it, even if it does not interfere in the field of their competence or compromise their responsibilities. The experience offers students an interesting possibility of development and represents a significant turn in education. It is a simple and correct proposal for environmental education, because it invites children to get to know the neighborhood directly, going through it every day, in the different seasons, to capture its details, its activities, its changes, the people that inhabit it. Small personal experiences that, taken to school and added together, can be an interesting base for learning and planning tasks.

It is also a concrete and serious experience of road education, also starting from individual daily experiences, to study together the best routes and the most appropriate behaviors, both for children and drivers.[11]

We asked teachers to assess the possibility of reducing the weight of the backpacks, looking into different modalities of study in class and for homework: leaving, for example, some books at school and others at home.

The parents

We believe it is important to give parents the possibility of discovering their children's capacity for self-control and responsibility, which will certainly be greater than what they imagine, and of recovering for themselves greater

---

[11] See file n.10: "A pedestrian, cyclist and motorcyclist card".

autonomy, more time, less ties, freeing themselves from the obligation of accompanying them every day. With them, the most difficult confrontation occurred, with respect to what they considered a serious danger to their children. It was agreed, however, that the greatest danger is represented precisely by their cars, which, at that time, were responsible for much of the traffic around the schools. We reasoned together about the need for children to find forms of solidarity (going to pick up other classmates, accompanying each other) and greater autonomy. That they experience the different seasons of the year without fear of rain or snow (always considered pleasant events in our childhood). Finally, it was arranged, without being able to make it obligatory, of course, that children should be allowed to go to school and return home alone within a defined area,[12] so that those who lived far away would be accompanied to this limit and not to school.

Many parents asked that some urban improvements be made before the experience began which would make the critical points of the two neighborhoods safer, but we agreed that this would take too much time to start the experience and that we would have more strength before the administration if we ask for improvements with experiences that had already been initiated; with the children in the streets and after having registered the real demands and priorities. Naturally, not everyone was convinced.

The elderly

We went to the elders' associations not to ask them to assume a particular role of vigilance or assistance but, as we said before, to ask them to "be", to go out in these time slots, to walk, to read the newspaper on a bench, to go shopping; in short, to be alert and to be the grandparents of all the children.

The vendors

This category has a feature that makes it significant for this experience: the vendor is on the street and therefore has the children in sight; and, as he is always there, he can become a point of reference. We asked the shopkeepers of the two neighborhoods to participate in the project, and those who joined (almost all) displayed a sticker in their shop windows. Children know the symbol and know that, where it appears, they can enter and telephone home without paying for the call, drink water, pee, or resolve a conflict.

---

[12] It would correspond more or less to the area of influence of the school, and its limits would not exceed 500-700 meters of radius, which would be the maximum distance that a student would go alone from their educational center.

This resource was used very little, perhaps because in reality the journey did not present difficulties, perhaps because the children wanted to show us their autonomy. When they were in need of it, they used it with their own and the merchants' full satisfaction.

The teenagers

Then, we had a meeting with the high-school students near the elementary schools. The parents had expressed their fear of the students' motorcycles and the possible inconvenience that these could cause. We found instead a lot of attention and willingness to collaborate and favor this small but important experience of their younger schoolmates.

Traffic Department

The initiative was launched in collaboration with the Traffic Department, which used experimental street signs to warn motorists that children go to school unaccompanied in that area. The Traffic Department also promoted an update course for the local police officers called "The local police, a friend of the children".

Poster made by the Traffic Department of Fano to delimit the area where the experience was carried out. "We go to school by ourselves. Attention - Children crossing".

The motorists

Through the appropriate road signs, motorists were informed of the experience, offering them a wonderful educational opportunity in respecting the rights of pedestrians.

The neighborhood

The initiative, in addition to offering children an opportunity for autonomy, wants to return the street experience of the children to the neighborhood. An experience that is not intended to provoke romantic memories, but to prepare a sustainable future, with less pollution, less noise, with more security, and more people on the street.

Some data

The "Let's go to school alone" initiative was preceded or associated with research activities that aimed to collect information or assess the first results of the experience. In Fano, the investigation began at the end of the first year of the launch of the initiative (1995), while in Palermo and in Rome, it was done at the beginning.

Fano

Before the end of the school year, four months after launching the initiative, a questionnaire was proposed to the students and parents of the two participating schools to find out if they had changed the way they go to school, if they were satisfied with the experience and what difficulties and proposals they could point out. 385 students (interviewed at school) and 316 parents responded. Their responses are substantially similar after calculating the average. We will only give information on the activity evaluation here.

Before the initiative, 68% of the students went to school accompanied by car, 12% accompanied on foot by adults and 20% on foot unaccompanied. Naturally, these percentages vary according to the different school levels: in fifth grade, 50% of the students went to school alone.

After launching the initiative, only 20% of the students continue to be driven to school, while 76% go unaccompanied.

Naturally, climatic conditions have a significant impact on the autonomy of children and only 33% of them go to school alone when it rains.

The vast majority of respondents, 95% of children and 87% of parents, make a positive evaluation of the experience. The predominant motivations of this satisfaction, in the following order, are: the increase of autonomy, the possibility of knowing the city, the pleasure of meeting friends (conformation given, above all, by children). The most cited motivations to justify the negative responses are: danger, discomfort (confirmed by children), the weight of backpacks. The most cited proposals to improve the safety of the house-school route were: greater vigilance on the part of the police, greater guarantees (separation of cars) in the pedestrian crossing areas and in the bicycle lanes. These proposals for greater defense and separation are more frequent among parents, while children are more interested in greater respect for their rights by adults and, in particular, by motorists.

Palermo

In Palermo, two neighborhoods, one in the suburbs and one in the center, had been chosen for the implementation of the initiative that included 3,550 parents and 3,550 students from primary and secondary schools. The questionnaires sought to uncover how the children make the home-school journey, the evaluation of the proposal to go alone and on foot, and the possible difficulties and proposals.

The questionnaires were distributed at school and answered at home, both by the parents and by the students, with a return percentage of almost 50% (the low percentage depends both on the way the questionnaire was distributed and the absence of awareness prior to the initiative).

In high school, 40% of the students are accompanied by car; the percentage rises 58% on rainy days. 16% are accompanied on foot.

37% go to school unaccompanied and on foot; 7% of the students go by bus.

In elementary school, the percentages are different: 44% are taken by car and 40% of the children go on foot, accompanied by an adult. 16% of the students go to school alone and walk.

66% of children and 54% of parents declare themselves in favor of the initiative and set out the need for greater autonomy as the predominant motivation.

34% of the children and 46% of the parents declare themselves, on the contrary, against; exposing the danger of the traffic and the social risks, the distance of the school and the weight of the backpacks as predominant motivations.

Rome

In Rome, the project was taken by District V and was applied in some of its neighborhoods with the name "The neighborhood of the children". The investigation was carried out in two neighborhoods, in which the activity "Let's go to school alone" began.

With respect to the other cities, the research in Rome was carried out with strong scientific support and using a complex and articulated questionnaire, via a system of interviews conducted by a research team.[13] The interviews included an experimental sample of 400 children from the last elementary and high school courses. The questions in the questionnaire referred to different topics, including child mobility for the home-school journey. The collected data concluded that 68% of the students go to school accompanied by adults, either by car or on foot; 13% of the children always go to school alone and 18% only occasionally had the opportunity to make the journey without being accompanied.

Children prefer to be accompanied because their parents are afraid (67.2%) and, to a lesser extent, because they are small (18.8%).

The majority of children who are accompanied declare themselves able to go to school alone (76.2%).

The greatest difficulty that children point out regarding their experience of autonomy is their fear of "dangerous people," who they identify with the marginal groups: homeless people and beggars, gypsies, drug addicts, thieves, kidnappers. Less disturbing to them are the dangers derived from traffic and they consider them, instead, as a predominant fear of adults.

Conclusions

As the data from Palermo and Rome show, most children want greater autonomy, they consider themselves capable of facing the test of going to school without the company of adults. The strong presence of fear linked to the social dangers of the environment is interesting and disturbing, certainly conditioned by the recommendations of adults and the information from the media, but which also partly reflect the deteriorating situation of the suburban areas. Children are less worried about the dangers of traffic. Faced with this situation, the implementation of this initiative seems even more urgent, which will help children and parents to build a more serene neighborhood environment and contribute so that the danger, which can still exist, is reduced to controlled and acceptable levels.

Fano's experience, which continues to have a substantial positive response from families and children since March 1995, demonstrates that fears can be banished only with experience. In Fano, the parents were also afraid of both traffic and social dangers, but once the experience was launched, almost all adults and children declared themselves satisfied.

---

[13] The research in Rome was directed by Dr. Vittoria Giuliani, a researcher at the Institute of Psychology of the CNR, an expert in environmental psychology.

Children, in particular, recognize that they go to school more at ease and, according to the testimony of one of the two educational directors, they are more punctual when they go to school alone. Two consequences that do not seem minor.

The fragility of experiences such as this one, which require non-negligible changes in family habits, must be stressed. The City Council, which asks children to go to school alone, asks parents not only to have confidence in their children but also in the behavior of other adults, motorists, passers-by, vendors. Naturally, if a City Council asks for this, it must commit itself to do everything in its power to ensure the greatest safety of our children. Families rely on this favorable attitude and ask for measures that increase security. If these measures are not taken, especially if they have been promised, trust in the Administration falls apart and the children return to school by car.

This has happened in some way in Fano, during the second year, with the participation in the experience decreasing precisely because of the delays in the completion of the work requested by the citizens that the Administration had promised. Again, the problem of timing, again the need to consider the project as a profound transformation, not only in the things still to be done but also in the sensitivity that is reflected in the procedures.

10. A pedestrian, cyclist and motorcyclist card

A road safety education proposal

The local councils have expertise in road education and allocate funds to the acquisition of materials such as brochures, notices, videos. Materials that allow teachers to give their usual classes with more images, but the objective of this economic and organizational effort remains unchanged – that the students know the signs and the main articles of the Highway Code as early as possible. To make this operation more credible and more effective, police officers are invited more and more frequently to the classes, so that they are the ones who teach the code and the signs, even if they have no experience teaching children. These activities are destined to a profound failure for several reasons. First of all, it does not seem reasonable to teach traffic signs and the Highway Code to children of the ages of eight or ten, who still have several years before they can drive a car; it is not true that the increase in information and knowledge ensures the change in behavior (young people, for example, continue smoking although they know all the statistics of the risks they are running). At school, therefore, we study how we should behave in the street, while on the street adults behave as if they have never been to school, and children continue to move inside cars that drive these uneducated adults.

Hence, the Laboratory's proposal for a true road-education experience, experienced by the children in the streets of the city and linked to satisfy, even if partially, their demand for autonomy: "Let's go to school alone".

In support of the experience, it is proposed that courses for the "pedestrian" card in primary school, "cyclist" card in the first cycle of secondary school and "motorcyclist" card in the upper cycle of secondary school are organized. The idea is simply to strengthen the attention and commitment of children and young people and to increasingly engage the city in this operation aimed at making healthier behaviors and habits.

Pedestrian card

In elementary school, there could be courses promoted for '*the pedestrian card*' that plan the study of the route from home to school; the analysis of the best solutions in relation to time and security; the observation of motorists' behavior in matters such as speed, respect for pedestrian crossings, parking on sidewalks; and the identification of the highest risk points. After these inspections, which children may also carry out in the afternoon, proposal strategies and, if necessary, protest strategies must be developed, through the use of moral "fines"[14] and the request to the City Council for punitive or structural measures such as crossing changes, installation of traffic lights with alarm, etc.

Knowledge of the various components involved in the action of walking can be looked at in depth – the best position, the characteristics of the footwear, the weather of the different seasons and the best methods for moving freely or protecting against rain, heat, and snow, can be observed.

Children can take the role of "local police" to check the behavior of their peers and adults outside of school, taking note of the behavior they deem wrong. These will be discussed in class and, in case of serious situations in relation to motorists, submitting reports to the head of the local police may also be decided. Naturally, the objective is not to promote a kind of class leader, but to offer a different point of view that allows children to expose their demand for autonomy along with respect for the rules. Taking turns in this role-playing game systematically, and not for reasons of merit, will therefore be essential.

At the end of the course, there could be a big party, an obstacle course in the neighborhood square, where the traffic councilor delivers the pedestrian cards with a photo, stamps and postmarks. Then it will be important for the Administration to organize activities for the little "graduates", for example,

---

[14] See file n.8: "The fine of the children".

walks on Saturday or Sunday to visit interesting places from a natural or artistic point of view and share in a snack. During the holidays long trips on foot along interesting routes, following the guidelines of hiking can also be organized.

Cyclist card

In the city where the use of bicycles is possible, a "bicycle laboratory" could be opened in all secondary schools (this proposal in some positive environmental situations could also interest the last courses of primary school). A place where you can disassemble, clean, adjust, know the bicycle well. It is important that the school stimulates the students' passion for the bicycle, because our cities need to mold citizens who choose to leave the car at home and move without noise, without taking up much space, without unnecessarily ravaging non-renewable resources such as fuel, without polluting the air and damaging the works of art. On the other hand, the course for cycling cards should be developed like the pedestrian one; with the study of the region, the routes, demanding more attention from the Administration, as has been indicated several times in the other parts of the book. After the ceremony of presenting the cards, the Department of Traffic and the Department of Sports can organize walks, regular races, visits to interesting places of the surroundings for the "graduates" and, during the holidays, long bike trips broken up into stages.

Motorcyclist card

The motorcycle is, by the way, one of the myths of our teenagers. It is often the reason for great arguments with parents, it is the cause of non-irrelevant difficulties in urban circulation, it is responsible for a sharp increase in noise pollution and, unfortunately, is the cause of many, too many, head injuries that kill or paralyze young people and adolescents every day. The arrogance of the motorists is not the only thing to blame, accidents are often a consequence of young motorcyclists' bad habits. In addition to driving in a risky way, two people tend to use this so fragile vehicle, or ride without a helmet. The authorities responsible for the traffic tolerate these undesirable and dangerous habits in an incomprehensible and guilty way. However, if motorcycles were used correctly there would be notable benefits for the city, given that the space it occupies is five or six times less than that required by a car.

We propose the opening of a motorcycle laboratory in all secondary schools and in all centers where higher education is taught. It would be a place where students who have more problems in Greek and algebra would finally be at ease, but there could also be a technology workshop or a physics or chemistry laboratory, and so on. The viability of the city should be studied, satisfactory solutions for safe routes, and the construction of adequate parking proposed.

The risks and dangers should be studied to arrive together at the recognition of the need for proper driving, the use of helmets, and the impossibility of two traveling on a small motorcycle. Then, the students would be awarded the card and proceed to the social initiatives that follow; these could become meeting places where the correct public behavior would be reinforced.

It would be important for young people to understand that when they ride a motorcycle, they must respect the rights of the weakest, meaning both cyclists and pedestrians; the same respect that they ask of drivers.

This file was drafted in large part in a hypothetical way, as the proposal is still under review in schools. Its decision is expected to be settled upon it with the participation of the Department of Traffic, Sports, Education and sports associations and environmentalists; together with the Laboratory.

11. "My city and I"

An environmental education proposal

In 1993, the Fano Laboratory "The city of children" launched a proposal to all Italian schools which addressed the need to devote their attention to the increasingly difficult relationship between the child and the city; with the project "My city and me."

The plan, which covers several years, invites Italian students of any level to analyze an aspect of their city each year. With this analysis, they meet in Fano to get to know each other and compare their developed tasks. A great international congress is planned for the year 2000 in which, the aspects that were studied over several years are coordinated, the city is discussed according to the perspectives, expectations and proposals of children and young people.

We believe that this initiative represents a good environmental education program, especially for its proposal of knowing the region, of future planning, and perspectives. On the other hand, since the city is the place of greatest deterioration, urgent measures are required to stop it. It is in the city that the greatest attacks on the environment are carried out; it is from within it that an environmental "rebirth" can be initiated. Therefore, the Ministry of the Environment has recognized the Fano Laboratory as a territorial laboratory for environmental education, and the Ministry of Public Education, since its first year, has endorsed and spread the project "My city and me" through school newsletters.

In this and similar cases, there is one more value that must be taken into account – the children design real spaces of the city, they propose them to adults who should consider them more, modifying the traditional planning parameters of the city, based only on economic criteria and, always, with interest and relevance for adults only. These proposals therefore become effective environmental awareness initiatives for adults through children.

The themes

The theme proposed in the 1993-1994 school year was "The squares and monuments". Students were invited to answer the questions: "What is a square used for?"; "How should a square be made and equipped?"; "Where could a square like the desired one be built?"; "What does a monument mean?"; "Who would you make it for and how?".

The theme of the 1994-1995 course was "Let's recover the green". The proposal was to locate the pieces of land and plots where spontaneous vegetation grows, especially in the peripheral neighborhoods, whose ownership is unknown and which tend to become small, uncontrolled landfills; recovering their public use through proper planning.

The theme of the 1995-1996 course was "The streets and cars: we go to school alone", which studied the difficulties of urban mobility for the weakest citizens and possible solutions to increase their autonomy and counteract the excessive power of cars. "Garbage" is the work theme for the year 1996-1997 and issues for the coming years may be: "The school we want" and "Where to play?".

The method

Schools interested in the project send a membership form to the Fano Laboratory. They then respond to the classes with a methodological document, specially prepared each year, which suggests some activities on the proposed topic.

It is argued that schools must develop the topic, with full freedom in expressive forms and languages. It is proposed to start the work with concrete, real experiences: the individualization of a neighborhood space, or the identification of a problem to be overcome. This is the starting point for collecting information, understanding the ownership of the area, and formulating transformation hypotheses. In the elaboration of a project, using the advice and collaboration of specialists from outside the school is suggested; helping the students take the norms, the characteristics of the materials, and possible solutions into account. They may be City Council specialists or architects, urban planners, naturalists, etc.

It will be important, both for the educational aspects and for the greater feasibility of the work, for the class to also study the materials and the costs that it demands; assessing which operational contribution the students themselves, parents, and grandparents can make, as much for the realization as for the maintenance. The work will end with the preparation of a project and, if possible, with a model that will be presented to the appropriate councilors.[15]

The Fano week

Every year, during the month of April, the closing week of the project "My city and I", dedicated to children, is celebrated in Fano. During this time, classes and groups (if it is about associations) that have participated send, or personally show, their projects.

The highlight of this week is a great exhibition of the projects and models made by children from different cities on the theme proposed for that year. A second exhibition consists of the best posters that Fano's children have made for the poster contest of the year.[16] To these other samples organized by the Laboratory, by national or local associations or by the elders of the city are added. In the six years of activity, among others, the sample of Reggio Emilia children's schools "The hundred languages of children" and the exhibition organized by Mario Lodi on children's drawing have been presented in Fano.

Every day of the week shows are offered by various theater groups, local or of other cities, of children or for children, in the morning in the schools and in the afternoon in the squares, and theaters of the city.

Various meetings or congresses are also held during the week. One, perhaps the most representative, is that of the project-executing children, during which the authors discuss the work they have exhibited in the model with colleagues in different cities and the adults. The children of the Fano Council coordinate and direct this meeting respecting the expected times which always surprises the adults. In any case, they are thinking of changing this presentation, which runs the risk of imitating the congresses of adults too much and attracting little interest among the children who attend, especially those who still have to take part. Exhibiting the projects in a much larger space is also planned, as well as inviting the groups to explain their work at different times of the day.

Another congress organized is that of the administrators; on the theme of the year and its educational and urban implications. The appointment with the administrators is an important one which allows an exchange of experiences between the interested cities and those already engaged in this project. In recent years, another in-depth meeting has been added to the April meeting, which is held in December.

---

[15] See also file n.4: "The project-executing children"
[16] See file n.12: "My city and I": the poster.

There have also been meetings with the teachers on topics closer to the methodology of the proposal (from environmental education to collaboration with specialists who do not belong to the school) and with the architects on the different aspects of the architecture shared with the children.

For a week, many important and prestigious places in the city are "left" to the children; for their meetings, their shows, their models. The stores display their posters, the radio and the local press take care of them. For a week, the city becomes a little more of a city of children.

On Sundays, the city is closed to the circulation of vehicles[17] and is left available to children as "a city to play with." Every year the children are allowed to use the various urban spaces as playgrounds: the squares and alleys of the historic center as surprising stages for theatrical shows; the sand as material for different recreational activities – to make volcanoes, castles, ramps, for bowling. The pebbles of the stony beach are used as materials for original compositions or paintings, or to start the search for the most rounded pebble; the city walls and bastions also become huge toys. In recent years, since the children achieved the closure of the city to the circulation of cars, the street has become an ideal place for games, and symbolizes the desire of all citizens, starting with children, to retake the city.

Some data

The participation in the week has been variable, very much conditioned by the moment in which the ministerial notice arrived at the schools and by the concurrence of general or municipal elections in the week of April that in Italy, unfortunately, have been a constant in the last three years. Despite these difficulties, about fifty schools (on average) have sent projects to Fano and several municipal administrations of their representatives. More than ten Italian regions, and some foreign delegations, were always represented.

The number of models sent to Fano has constantly increased compared to the number of traditional posters; which were the predominant material of the first years. This means that the schools are accepting the work indications proposed by the ministerial notice and the methodological document sent by the Fano Laboratory: operational intervention in the territory, collaboration with specialists outside the school, and the use of new technologies such as the realization of models.

---

[17] See also file n.13: "A day without cars".

The high participation of projects, children, teachers and administrators, despite the fact that the expenses were borne by the participants and the "political" difficulties of the recent years mentioned before, demonstrates the recognition of the importance not only of the methodological proposal, but also of the occasion of real encounter of children and adults around the exhibited works and the occasion to "play" together in the city.

12. "My city and I": the poster

Posters chosen as a symbol of the 1995 and 1996 campaigns. Michela, three years old, of the Arco Iris nursery, in Fano, made the one of 1996. On the left: "The streets and the traffic"; on the right: "Me and my city: give us the green".

Three years ago, the poster of the national initiative "My city and I" originated from a contest held between children and teenagers in the schools of Fano. The Laboratory distributed a 100x70 cm plain white poster in the schools, only with the graphic symbol of the campaign and the titles. Children painted the poster freely, representing the theme of the year, choosing their preferred technique, working from home or in school, individually or in a group. All the presented posters, always more than one hundred, were submitted to a commission; formed by the professors of the Institute of Art and the Pedagogical high school, a graphic artist and the scientific director of the Laboratory, who selected those that would be exhibited during the April week and chose the one that seemed the most suitable to represent the theme of the year. This was printed and became the symbol of the project – it was the prize for the little author. All the posters that weren't used for the exhibition were displayed in the store windows.

13. A day without cars

As reminded in the file "The Municipal council, open to children", during the extraordinary meeting in 1993, it was asked for cars to be less invasive, to take less space that children can play. The councilor for traffic, in an outburst of generosity, promised that he would close the entire city to cars for a whole day. The difficulties arose later, because it was not a question of only closing a street or a square, but a city with important streets and high-traffic intersections; such as the Adriatic and Flaminia. But the promise was made and the Laboratory was firm in asking that it be fulfilled. The promise was kept, authorization was requested from the civil government, the necessary deviations were foreseen and established, and the streets were handed over to the children to play.

In the extraordinary meeting of the municipal plenary of Fano of 1994, the children asked to increase the number days in which the streets were closed to the cars. The Councilor for Traffic did not make risky promises this time, but he could not go back on the commitment he made the previous year, and thus the closing day has been confirmed over the last three years and is now a wonderful tradition.

> "Today the streets of Fano are closed to cars because they have given themselves to the children to play."

Since then, on the closing Sunday of the "My city and I" campaign,[18] children, as well as adults, retake the streets that, from prohibited and

---

[18] See file n.11: "My city and I".

dangerous places, become privileged spaces for playing. It is unusual, but full of meaning, to watch children and adults walk in a row along the dividing line of the lanes, towards the discovery of a new freedom. The street becomes the place of the different traditional games, of theater, of the parade on stilts. Groups of entertainers and female students from the Pedagogical High School help children "discover" old street games or propose new activities. The street becomes a large blackboard, the length of a city, where paths and play spaces or images are drawn, like those that are drawn in chalk on the pavement by street artists. When the motorists, who have the "luck" to drive in Fano on this day, find the street closed and are forced to look for a detour, an unpleasant pursuit by the way, they face a sign that says:

Our hope is that these motorists, together with their valid annoyance at the prolongation of their trip, can carry with them, as stimuli for reflection, thoughts of this type: "But how strange these people of Fano are, playing in the street ... although when I was little ... and why not also my son? ...".

Closing the streets for a day is undoubtedly just a symbol, a gesture, but gestures are also important because they help us believe in new things. They are small caresses that help to hope. They help children grow with these desires; they help adults break habits that are often confused with needs.

14. A seal of quality for children in hotels and restaurants

Restaurants and hotels also custom-made for children

The project, as previously mentioned several times, covers the entire city, all its aspects, all its structures, which undergo a critical review based on the demands of the children.

Fano is a tourist beach town that families primarily frequent. That is why the Tourism Promotion Agency was interested from the beginning in the emergence of the Laboratory; they supported it and expressed a willingness to propose a series of suggestions to restaurant, hotel and campsite owners to make their facilities more suitable for children. After several meetings with the mayor, councilors of the corresponding areas, Tourism Promotion Agency and owners, the proposal took shape at the meetings of the Children's Council.

Children's proposals

The following proposals arose directly and without adult intervention in a session of the Fano Laboratory Children's Council, after the counselors gathered the ideas in the respective schools.

To make a restaurant suitable for children

Lucia: movable windows that are removed in summer and put back in winter, with self-service so that children can do it themselves.

Beatrice: Of 90 children, 30 children wanted good food that they liked; 14, park and playroom; 13, a garden; 12, low and wide tables; 10, no smoking; 6, fast service, friendly staff and clean bathrooms.

M. Vittoria: Near the restaurant a room for children, so they do not have to stay at the table waiting for the adults and getting bored; dress casually; wall paintings

Massimo: Prepare the menu and cook; decide how much food you want.

Nicola: Dining room only for children with fixed benches to the wall and floor to avoid falls.

Francesca: Hard and washable plastic dishes with cartoon characters.

Chiara: Smoking room because children are bothered by tobacco and it harms us; after lunch, free candy and a whole room to play.

Dennis: Friendly and ingenious waiters, gym with small soccer fields.

To make a hotel suitable for children

Lucia: Toy-shaped structure with many toys inside.

Elena: I would like more control in the garden, TV rooms, free games, self-service, a mini-library. Babysitters for parents who want to go out and do not know where to leave the children.

Giorgia: We would like parks with games, a swing and others, swimming pools and game rooms, and also paper to draw.

Beatrice: TV in the room with cartoons for children, with non-flammable furniture and unbreakable decorations.

M. Vittoria: Large and colorful rooms with non-dangerous toys and with things a little messy. Strong beds that you can also jump on. Lower prices than the current ones because if not, we will not go again. A club for children with hobbies like dancing and going to the beach.

Massimo: Non-strict schedules. Choose silent activities instead of going to sleep, such as reading, drawing, dressing up, painting, preparing the menu and cooking. Keys for personal use. Handles and knobs, showers, switches, and mirrors, at the child's height. Movie theater, creative computers with three-dimensional images, being able to make music with instruments, moments of reading aloud.

Nicola: Space to play with tables and chairs without edges, a large television screen, computers, washable walls with paint brushes. Beds with protection against possible falls, consoles with games and soundproofed walls (to scream). "Neat" bathrooms. Garden with games, booths and a space for the little ones. Carpets, elevators for the disabled.

Margherita: There could be a mini-cinema where animated movies are played every two hours and a room with comics.

Francesca: Wardrobes for party dresses, guided walks for children on foot and with buses or special trains. Models of the most beautiful monuments of the city.

Manila: Adequate facilities for customers' animals.

Dennis: Garden with people who think about us.

Giacomo: Luxury hotel with a forest behind it and a small zoo, a small bar, a playground.

Laboratory's proposals

Based on the children's proposals, which show the main modifications that can transform these services into places that are also pleasant for them, the

Laboratory has formulated a series of proposals for tourism entrepreneurs and Fano's Tourist Promotion Office that they can discuss, and thus enrich each other.[19] If it is possible to establish a list of the conditions that a restaurant and a hotel must meet to adapt to what children want, a *Seal of Quality for Children* can be proposed from which the establishments that deserve it would benefit.

If a list of conditions is established detailing the requirements a restaurant or hotel must meet in order to be suitable for children, a *Seal of Quality for Children* can be proposed whereby the establishments that deserve it would benefit.

The seal may be awarded by a commission composed of representatives of the Tourist Promotion Office, the Laboratory, and the Children's Council. If the initiative thrives in Fano in the experimental phase, it can then be evaluated whether it should be implemented on a regional or broader scale.

The demand that arises more clearly from the children's proposals is that of a greater autonomy: in the use of services, in leisure, and with respect to adults.

Restaurants

Children know the restaurant better than the hotel and therefore the proposals are more complete and satisfactory.

A separate dining room or an independent corner in the common dining room with low and wide tables, suitable for children (maybe so several can eat together). Naturally, in this children's room or in their area smoking will be prohibited.[20]

Self-service so they can serve themselves, deciding the quality and quantity of food. You could think of a food presentation table, like a free buffet, so that children can see, choose and serve themselves.

Food suitable for children, but good, prepared in the most pleasant way for them. Children, for example, often refuse a steak or beefsteak, but they appreciate meatballs or hamburgers. Presenting food in such a way could improve the quality, excluding drinks and dishes that are not adequate: from soft drinks to spicy foods.

A fixed price could be established, so that neither children nor parents have to worry about this aspect.

Friendly and fun staff. This means that they would like some of the employees to know how to deal with them: cheerful staff, capable of joking, tolerant.

A place of entertainment to wait for the adults who continue chatting, without getting bored.

---

[19] The proposals of the children would deserve a much deeper analysis, distinguishing the trivial ones from some very innovative ones. Here we have just ordered them to make them a credible and acceptable proposal for restaurant and hotel owners.

[20] The availability of a separate space should not be understood as an obligation or as a suggestion for adults and children not to eat together, but as one more resource only. When we want to be with our children and they want to be with us, we will be sure to meet; when we want to talk to our friends without caring for children, it is better that they be with others of the same age.

The place can be outdoors in summer and covered in winter.
Being able to dress informally. Cheerful and pleasant decoration, so that children feel at ease.
Children's drawings and sculptures, provided by the principals of nursery schools, could be used in exchange for teaching materials.
Hygienic services, hangers, doorknobs, etc., tailored to children.

Hotels
Reserved TV room, with videotapes that children like. We think it is important that the TV is not connected to television channels, but only works with videotapes. This would avoid unsuitable, or simply unattractive, shows and the onslaught of commercials. Small users can therefore choose autonomously. The TV may be available only for a few hours to avoid excessive television passivity.
Playroom and library. A corner of the room can house a small library. The books should preferably be from children's literature (from picture books for the little ones to the first novels); children should be able to read alone, or have adults read to them. Books can be consulted or borrowed, with the minimum possible formality (for example, by filling in a simple form). The playroom and the library can share the television space, taking advantage of different schedules or different areas of the same room.
Non-strict schedules. The hotel, which for adults is the place of freedom, usually does not change the children's habits or makes them even stricter, for example, the nap obligation. The possibility of using their own spaces could make children's schedules and habits freer.
With regard to the rooms, taking the characteristics and needs of children into account is proposed: doorknobs, switches, showers, mirrors at the child's height; a lamp near the bed; strong beds to jump on.
The hotel should take care of its interior decoration so that children feel accepted, expected, almost like at home. Together with the paintings, those decorative elements chosen with the adult public in mind, we must also consider ornaments that are close to the world of children (as has already been said about the restaurant).
Provide a babysitting service so that parents have the freedom to go out at night. An assistance service for children could also be organized collectively, using common spaces.
Animations and traveling shows between the different hotels (puppets, theater, guided visits to the city, etc.), in collaboration with the Laboratory, can be considered and organized.
By working in collaboration with the departments of tourism and education, the Tourist Promotion Office, hotel managers, and the Laboratory, some playgrounds and activities for children should be organized by the sea, as an alternative and a support for beach activities.[21]

---

15. A beach for the children

Many times, the child gets bored on the beach. It would like to get in the water at every possible moment, but adults don't allow it. It gets tired of the sand, it gets tired of the sun, it doesn't know what to do. It asks for suggestions and help from parents, who only seem interested, however, in

---

[21] See file n.15: "A beach for the children".

sunbathing as much as possible or in continuing the talk or games with adults under the beach umbrella.

It would be important that beach establishments devote their attention to the needs of the children; they would therefore respect the little ones' right to play and have fun and increase the well-being of the elderly.

For some years, the Fano Laboratory has been presenting a series of proposals that aim to make the beach a suitable place for children to the owners, the Tourist Promotion Office and the Department of Tourism. The following services should be provided as mandatory in the beach concession contracts. Their number would be established in relation to the beach huts or bathers.

- *Beach hut for babies.* A beach hut for babies should be made available to families, equipped with a bathtub, diapers, whatever is necessary to heat the bottle and a fridge.

- *Playhouse.* Beach huts with comics, books, drawing materials and toys, to lend to children on the beach. The provision of these beach huts could be considered in collaboration with the Department of Educational Policy.

- *Beach huts and bathrooms for the disabled.* Beach huts and bathrooms with large doors and handles to facilitate the movement of people in wheelchairs, making it pleasant to change and use the services.

- *Descent to the sea by wheelchair.* At least one ramp on each beach should be built, which allows the disabled to go down to the sea with a suitable chair and the necessary assistance.

- *Areas equipped for children.* In addition to the services mentioned above, which must be managed directly by license holders on the beach, we have proposed to provide each section of a beach with sectors equipped for children. These would be areas controlled by entertainers, where children, who did not want to sunbathe or be in the sand or with adults all the time could walk freely and do the activities they wanted. The area may include a library area, a playground, creative painting and molding activities, free spaces for small theater and puppet shows that may be offered periodically. Typical craft workshops in the city could also be included. In the case of Fano, they can, for example, propose workshops with stone, cardboard and masks directed by the "float masters" of the local Carnival Society; the weaving of nets under the guidance of old sailors; the construction of wicker baskets, typical ceramics, etc.

The children have prepared projects in two of these areas that are awaiting the approval and completion of the City Council technical office. They are creative projects that use the available space by appropriately adapting its use to the environmental characteristics.

16. The COC club

During these years, the city of Fano has been enriched by an increasing number of children and young people who, after having actively participated in the projects of "The city of children", have developed a special relationship with the city and have become aware of citizen rights, especially those belonging to the smallest. This is the case of those who had been advisors, architects, and guides. This is about a hundred young people who are in high school and who are at risk of losing the interest and enthusiasm they had acquired. We consider this a luxury that the city cannot afford to lose, because these young people will soon be parents and could be the future administrators. If we lose contact with them, it will be easy to find them either as anxious parents, forgetting their children's needs, or as inattentive administrators.

Often these young people return to the Laboratory to find out if we are organizing something for them, or if they can help with something. We have then thought about opening a COC (City of Children) club that has its own organization and its own independent headquarters; with one of their purposes being to offer the Laboratory voluntary collaboration and help. Club supporters could be a "support unit" for our battles, acting within the middle and high schools; our reinforcements in the organization of the week in April and the meetings with the mayors; the privileged allies of the youngest children in the different experiences of autonomy, from going to school alone to free play in the afternoon.

The COC could also deal with the sale of products linked to "The city of children" (t-shirts, notebooks, posters, stickers), to support the initiatives and obtain a small fund that can be managed independently. Both the fact of having a headquarters to meet and having enough autonomy to organize themselves, coordinated by an adult who is not controlling or influencing their decisions, seem to me to be the necessary conditions for young people to continue being citizens and protagonists of our cities.

This project is currently under study in the Laboratory and in the Department of Social Policies.

17. The Archilei house

An orchard restored to the city

The economic and cultural history of Fano is linked to the port and the orchards. While the port has continued to have some importance and is now undergoing restoration, the allotments, due to their unfortunate location beyond the city limits, have become desirable spaces for building and are gradually disappearing. The Archilei House was precisely one of these allotments, one hectare, which had been rendered useless and surrounded by urbanization. Municipally owned, the Regulatory Plan had allocated it to the area of civil buildings. It could therefore become an interesting source of income for the local authority.

When the Laboratory "The city of children" was born, the Archilei House was assigned to some associations for the defense of nature; to use it as a venue for educational activities while negotiating its sale to some real estate agency as a building plot.

The associations and the Laboratory put pressure on the Administration so that this garden would be saved from urbanization and destined for children and education. After long discussions and several battles in the City Council, the requalification of the land as a green area for public use was obtained. An important result, in total contrast to the usual trend – the local authority knew how to give up a sure economic interest to give the city an educational resource. The option also indicates a line of development that all cities should adopt – all spaces forgotten by the savage urbanization of the last decades should be linked and allocated for social uses such as squares and gardens, with timely revisions of the general regulatory plans.

Today, the Archilei House is a center of environmental education and defense of nature available to children. Several natural ecosystems have been rebuilt, such as a pond, a meadow, a forest (with trees planted and cared for by children), as well as the vegetation of the different areas of the region and a part of the allotment allocated for cultivation. In the old farmhouse studios have been set up for work with classes, for activities with educators, and a small rural museum.

In the Archilei House, members of the environmental associations and some young people who substitute the social service (conscientious objectors) work as volunteers. The center offers guided tours and days of scientific and naturalistic work to schools of various levels, from Fano and the Marche region. It is frequented by more than a thousand students per year.

18. A free afternoon for children

As has been said several times, the practical objective of the project "The city of children" is that the children are able to leave home alone. The proposal to go to school alone is the first step, the most controllable and easiest in which to make a crack in the hard shell of fear, of suspicion, which produce selfishness and isolation.

While we continue to insist that the experience of going to school alone become widespread quickly, we must launch proposals for children's free time, to expand it and make it truly "free". One way of experimenting on this important front may be to offer children one afternoon per week, to be used with complete autonomy. For this to be possible, a kind of social pact must be made among adults.

If the chosen afternoon were, for example, Wednesday, for that occasion, the family should not enroll their children in any extracurricular activities, schools should not give homework, parishes should not teach catechism courses. Naturally, the Laboratory will also have to refrain from any organized activities of entertainment or games, because otherwise, we would transform "free" time into "organized" time. The city should be asked, instead, to be available and welcoming to the children, accepting them in their public spaces and "keeping an eye" on them. Therefore, the attention of the elderly, young people, local police officers and shopkeepers should be counted on, as stated by the experience "Let's go to school alone."

On this afternoon, at least in an experimental sense, free or discounted tickets could be given to children on public transport, favoring their use and access to knowledge of the different parts of the city.

It will be interesting to see if on that afternoon the children take advantage of the proposal by leaving the TV. If so, the children will confirm, without a shadow of a doubt, the effective and correct weapon against the supreme power of this intrusive appliance.

19. A stone garden

Also without green

It has often occurred to me to hear concerns of the type: "The problem for the child is not only leaving home, but also where to go to play: the nearest garden or meadow is more than half an hour away on foot and it can't go there alone". I do not know if it is a consequence of the just ecological battles or again because of the strange effect of the tendency of adults to quickly forget their childhood experiences, that this strange idea that a green space is needed to play has been affirmed. But children are not a herd of goats. They know how to play in any environment as long as they are left with a little freedom, a little time, and a little space. It is they who know what, with what, and how to play, it is not a matter for the adults. It is good to play in the street, in the squares, around the monuments, as well as in the gardens and parks. Anywhere can be played, obviously in a different way.

FRATO 96

Logo of the Laboratory "The city of children" of Palermo.

I often remember that I was fortunate to have been a child in the early postwar years and to have had, as privileged places to play, bombed houses. The ruins mark places abandoned by adults that therefore become magical places for children to play. They are places that lose their initial characteristics and can become, through children's fantasy, forts, forests, houses... They are abandoned places.

Palermo is a city that has "known" to preserve the ruins of the war until today in its historic center. It has not been, by the way, a choice of adults in favor of children, nor does the city intend to keep this haunting inheritance. However, in my recent role as advisor to the mayor of this fascinating city, for the project "The city of children", I proposed to offer the children from the center one, or some of, these ruins; turning them into "stone gardens" and at the same time a memory of a tragedy that is important not to forget.

It is about bringing the demolished walls to a height compatible with security, of restoring the space to make it usable, of creating, in short, a kind of maze of walls, doors, windows, a place to invent environments, scenarios, games. Between the walls, pavements, steps, grassy areas, benches, and plants can be alternated.

A destroyed place can be dignified and returned to the creative play of children, to the quiet rest of the elderly, and to the meeting of lovers.

Today, this is the undisputed kingdom of the street children, but it could be the land of their freedom, in addition to becoming the meeting place with other children, those who today live in their expensive apartments. As stated in the second part, we must attempt, before we begin to take the children from the street to school or to other institutions which are strange and often hostile for them, to improve their usual environment, to encourage their encounters with other children, so that afterwards, starting from a situation of security and privilege for the most problematic, they will want to go together, even in organized environments, and share educational experiences.

20. Other experiences: the planning shared with the children

Interview with Raymond Lorenzo[76]

How was the idea of including citizens, especially children, in the development of projects for the city obtained?

Before starting our talk, it should be noted that I know the American situation above all, and I will refer to it more than anything else. In the United States, the first experiences of shared planning go back to the sixties and were carried out by citizen movements, which were coordinated and supported by university professors from the architecture and urban planning faculties. In general, they originated from decayed neighborhoods, in response to intervention plans in the city proposed by the central government, and did not allow for child participation. In many cases, specialists and citizens organized themselves into committees or self-development cooperatives, and thanks to central government funding, permanent structures emerged; the Community Designer Centers which still carry out these activities.

---

[76] Raymond Lorenzo is an urban planner, technical coordinator of the WWF campaign "Re-conquer the city", consultant for the *Istituto degli Innocenti* for the project "The urban child", and an associate member of the Children's Environment Research Group in New York.

At the same time, various investigations concerning children and the urban environment were aimed at studying the demands of children in cities and communicating the results of these investigations to urban planners and administrators.

When did the idea of including children in urban planning activities appear?

One must wait for the beginning of the seventies, when Robinson parks appeared in the UK and the United States; self-built spaces, planned together with children and young people. Robin Moore[77] and others were trying to transfer the adventure, nature and active play that were missing, or could not take place in the urban environment, to these parks.

In the same period, together with Florence Ladd[78] and Mark Francis,[79] I participated in the opening of laboratories in the poorest areas of the city of Boston; where methodologies that allowed children to study the urban environment and participate in the elaboration of the project were trialed.

Can you point out particularly significant facts that have helped affirm the shared planning?

The Children Nature Congress and the Urban Environment, which dates back to 1975, in which almost all the people who developed research activities in this field met, surely represents a very important moment. Roger Hart,[80] one of the organizers, asked me to coordinate, together with Mark Francis and Simon Nicholson,[81] the participation of children in the congress which was a revolutionary act. The children studied the city and we prepared a report on their understanding of the urban environment to present at the congress. At the same time, we opened a laboratory where children worked to ensure an

---

[77] Robin Moore is a professor of landscape architecture and president of the IPA (International Player Association)

[78] Florence Ladd deals with environmental psychology.

[79] Mark Francis is a professor of landscape architecture at Davis University in the state of California.

[80] Roger Hart, editor of Children's' Environment magazine.

[81] Simon Nicholson, passed away in 1990, was a professor of technology at the Oxford Open University. His publications *How Not to Cheat Children: The Theory of Loose Parts and Children as Planners* still represent an important theoretical reference for shared planning activities today.

exchange between them and the researchers. A strong message came out of the congress about the importance of including children in the drafting of projects which intend to transform the city.

In 1976, during the first Habitat Conference, a government trend emerged that recognized the importance of including citizens in city planning. The value of the contribution offered by the children was not established, but in the following years, a series of experiments were carried out that revealed the need for children to participate in the planning.

In which countries was the trend towards shared planning mainly established?

Several countries such as England, Austria and France are engaged in this type of activities. Manfred Drum, in Munich, has carried out with the Urbanes Wohnen association the highest number of initiatives born from shared architecture and urban planning projects across Europe. In the United States, there are very pragmatic laboratories that, in collaboration with the university, and sometimes including children, make proposals for the transformation of specific urban spaces.

How much does the fulfillment of projects affect activities that include children?

Undoubtedly, the fulfillment of the proposals is an important element, but I think that for children, the experience of participation, however, is valid. Participation contributes to a child's individual development because it allows them to feel like protagonists, converse with other citizens, acquire a longer lasting knowledge of their city; and everything is independent of the precision of the projects. The feasibility of their proposals is also discussed with the children leading to their awareness of the difficulties in their realization. The developed projects, in addition, have always been communicated to administrators and city specialists; enabling them to understand the children's needs.

Does shared planning also have positive consequences for the other citizens?

Children can teach adults many things about environmental management, especially from the perspective of sustainable development. Their projects propose measures that do not require substantial financing; natural elements are of considerable importance to them; they provide for the recovery of existing structures and, concerning materials, they favor the natural ones. All these elements, which are the basic principles of planning, are also present in the children's work, thanks to both their vision of the environment and our methodological orientation.

What elements represent an obstacle to the shared planning activities?

One of the difficulties is the parental intervention. Their fear for the inclusion of children in the preparation of proposals that will not be used afterwards is not entirely unfounded. The fall of a municipal government team, for example, can jeopardize the implementation of an approved project. Today, however, the distrust of citizens regarding the administration seems excessive. Another obstacle is the time required to carry out the projects, which without a doubt is too long. In addition, the approved proposal can also be modified when the executive project is defined and, consequently, the measures adopted may only partially reflect the suggestions made by the children. Another critical point is that of professionalism. In Italy, unlike the United States where the Community Design Centers have also had training activities for almost twenty years, there is a lack of interdisciplinary training necessary for the development of projects available to the professionals, but also there is a lack of artisanal professionalism, indispensable for its realization.

Can we end our interview trying to define what perspectives there are for this type of experience?

The outlook is unquestionably positive. Shared planning is no longer the typical and exclusive approach of childhood experts. Administrators show interest in the proposals children make; the National Urban Planning Institute is moving in the same direction. Gradually, the idea is spreading that other figures besides architects and urban planners are necessary to transform the urban environment.

21. Other experiences: the pedestrian rights

Interview with Dario Manuetti[82]

Can a city management policy that takes into account the rights of pedestrians contribute to the urban environment transformation process?

Today it can be said that the politics of mobility coincide with the politics of the city. Before, however, the concerns of those who designed the city mainly took into account residential and productive functions. Traffic moderation offers concrete solutions to the problems of mobility during the times of rush hour. The fundamental principle is that of the "democratization" of public space, of streets and squares, of the peaceful coexistence between cars and pedestrians.

What kind of measures are planned to moderate the traffic?

The opinion of experts in the European area, as well as the high number of accidents, indicate that psychological conditioning and educational action in response to motorists' behavior are not sufficient to guarantee the safety and mobility of all users of the public space. Physical conditions must be created so that cars move at a speed that is compatible with the characteristics of the urban environment.

The most visible action for moderating the movement of vehicles is to eliminate all architectural barriers for pedestrians and create them, instead, for cars. In the streets where the housing function predominates, it is suggested to narrow the lanes to expand the space of the sidewalk, to make the routes of the cars more complicated; putting obstacles on both sides of the street. Another important element is "vertical disengagement": elevating and lowering the level of cars at crosswalks, while pedestrians always move on the same level. This is obtained, for example, by creating pedestrian crossings a few centimeters above the level of the road.

---

[82] Dario Manuetti has been dedicated to the problems of the organization of culture, of permanent education, of the training of cultural and educational operators, as an associative activist, a municipal and public-entities administrator, and a consultant in municipalities and regions for twenty years. He is part of the management of the European Association for Social and Cultural Progress and is a member of the Regional Council on the problems of minors. He develops his professional activity in the Piedmont region, where he deals with social and professional orientation and integration.

In residential areas, where all the rules of traffic moderation, the characteristics of urban amenities and paving are applied, the environment is more pleasant and motorists' behavior is also modified. The road becomes a diverse space, where not only the presence of motorists is planned, but also that of children, the elderly, the disabled.

How was the idea of moderating traffic obtained?

Traffic moderation has a recognized historical origin in the city of Delft, in the Netherlands. In the seventies, a movement of citizens, supported by a municipal technical office that had a real availability to seek innovative solutions to problems related to mobility and pedestrian safety, conducted an extremely interesting experiment. Instead of spreading traffic lights, traffic signs, and local police through the city, demanding stronger sanctions, they introduced changes which were inconceivable until that point in the physical structure of the street; changes in motorists' culture and the attitude were also encouraged. These parents, citizens, and managers of the technical offices, going beyond the norms of the Code in force at that time in the Netherlands, took a series of measures that today represent the fundamental principles of the philosophy of traffic moderation. In 1976, the Dutch Traffic Code endorsed the fundamental rules of traffic moderation.

Which European countries have committed to this type of measures?

After the Netherlands, the second country that has faced the problem of mobility and, therefore, the rights of pedestrians in a fairly widespread and fast way is Germany. Other European countries such as Denmark, Austria, France and Switzerland are committed to sharing very interesting experiences.

How is Italy positioned in the European scene?

Italy, with respect to the European context, has a delay of almost twenty-five years which, in part, also derives from a late motorization of the masses. In the Netherlands, France, and Germany, widespread motorization was carried out in the fifties; therefore, they had time to assimilate to the novelty of the car. In these countries a research policy has been developed and, thanks also to the financing by the insurance companies, very interesting studies have been carried out on the relationship between the child and the car, on the possible links between aggressive and opportunistic behaviors, and use of cars or about the relationship between the child and the street. In Italy, we are in the beginning; in the phase of the first complaints of an intolerable situation. Only in recent years have we begun to face the problem of using the car in an "intelligent" way.

In addition to "The possible city", which proposes a wide range of actions, which associations face the problem of mobility?

Various environmental associations, beyond their capacity for deepening and continuing their actions, are engaged in projects that concern the issues of moderation. These are experiences that have a certain diffusion. As examples, we can remember the "Work in progress" program of the Legambiente and the project "The city reconquest" of the WWF.

Other associations, on the other hand, work on specific aspects of pedestrian mobility or protection, such as the Association of Parents of Injured Children, Assopedone, or Stradaamica, which is now a federation of four or five organizations at the national level and works primarily on the problem of street accidents. Another aspect that currently characterizes today's trend of associations is the requirement to join a common network, in which to consider the experience and have the possibility of comparing the national and international spheres. "The possible city" is working precisely in this direction.

What elements obstruct the spreading of moderation techniques?

The main difficulty is the lack of training. To change the city, it is not enough for citizens to inform on, and activate the demand for, urban quality; the responsiveness of administrators and specialists must also be increased. In Italy, there is a considerable delay with respect to other European countries because universities do not educate professionals in moderation techniques, and professional orders, in turn, have not developed a rigorous practice in bringing their specialists up to date.

Another obstacle derives from the behavior of motorists. Today cars allow higher and higher speed that can be reached in a short amount of time; including, therefore, in the urban space.

22. Other experiences: an emerging democracy

Interview with Carlo Pagliarini[83]

How were the municipal councils of children created in Italy?

The first experiences date back to the postwar period and were intended to allow the democratic organization of holiday communities.

In the sixties, children's councils were instituted in many municipalities, but these initiatives generally failed.

Most of the experiences of the current historical period are correlated with the initiative of the Italian Unicef "The mayor, defender of children". Some of the administrators who agreed have organized municipal councils for children. Many of these are totally deprived of cultural references and therefore reproduce the only model they know, that of the adult; others, on the other hand, represent high-quality experiences. In both cases, however, children express their potential and their competencies.

Where was the first Children's Council instituted?

In Morrovalle, and it is still in action. Although, in my opinion, it is an initiative that has only been carried out half-heartedly. The conviction that I have also implemented on the basis of the French experience is that the Municipal Council of Children must begin in the school, in relation, also, with the didactic programs, as an element of deep awareness of an active citizenship role; after which the activity must be carried out in the City Council through negotiations with adults. In Morrovalle, the Council remained within the school.

What are the most significant experiences?

In general, the presence and effectiveness of the Councils are linked to the nature of administration. When the municipal government is formed by people who do not come directly from the world of politics, there is an extraordinary mental openness towards these initiatives.

_____

[83] Carlo Pagliarini, founder and former president of Arciragazzi, founder of the Association "Democracia in erba" ("Emerging Democracy"), left us in 1997. Also, to him, who did so much for the children, I dedicate this book.

In your opinion, has the mayor's new role produced an increase in the formation of the Children's City Councils?

So far we have no records of this phenomenon because it is too recent, but I think so. Some mayors, for example, in their electoral program have planned the creation of a Children's Council.

What are the most significant experiences on the international scene?

France is the European country in which the experience of the children's councils has been most widespread. The phenomenon originated and developed in a phase of left-wing administration and also continued when the management of the municipalities passed to right-wing coalitions. This demonstrates the validity of the experience that is constantly growing – a year ago there were eight hundred, today they are eight hundred and sixty.

The French Children's City Councils appeared about ten years ago thanks to the initiative of a number of mayors. After this first spontaneous experience, some educational organizations and a group of administrators of large and small cities established an association, the ANACEJ (Association National des Conseils d´Enfants et des Jeunes) that today supports various ministries and institutions.

Initially, the Children's Councils were mostly created; recently, Youth Councils in which adolescents participate are being organized. Furthermore, th ese experiences mainly originate in small town halls where children are easily visible, and in turn, can easily adapt the region. Only one large city in France has a Children's City Council.

Thinking of big cities, in how wide an area should a Children's Council operate?

The ideal dimension, I think, corresponds to the area in use by a group of two or three schools. It must be an area that children know and in which they can take part in forms of planning and claiming their role. Only in this case, the City Council is valid; otherwise, it is a form of passive, symbolic participation, intended for adults rather than children.

What peculiarities does your proposal, that of "Emerging Democracy", have?
What distinguishes it, for example, from the French?

First of all, I must remember the enormous disproportion in the number of Councils and traditions, because in France there is an extraordinary secular educational network that we do not have. Italy completely lacks national and institutional support that instead characterizes the French situation.

We have gone against the tide and to some extent, we have been forced to make a more imaginative application.

If I must identify the differences between the two models, perhaps the main ones are the importance that we attach to the moments of play and to the organization of common assemblies, where adults and children debate together on a specific topic.

Can rules be defined that guarantee the effectiveness of a Children's council?

As the institution of the Councils is a recent phenomenon, it is not possible to give restrictive indications but to specify some aspects. The establishment of these experiences should be preceded by two formal acts: the adoption of the Convention on the Rights of the Child and a decree of the City Council, stating that children are citizens like others and, therefore, are granted power. Children's councils must have a budget to be able to exercise their functions with sufficient guarantees. The resources will be used in part for the functioning of the Council: for example, to travel, learn about other experiences or acquire skills; partly to take small interventions suggested by the children themselves.

Does "Emerging Democracy" also provide for the formation of an executive
committee that, as in France, promotes the development of the Council and
facilitates its activities?

Sure. According to "Emerging democracy", there must be at least three figures in the executive committee: a teacher representing the school or schools of a certain territory, an elder, who may have an experience of municipal management and who acts as a mediator between the children and the Council, and an entertainer.

Can there be situations in which the Children's Councils come to act in the territory by taking very circumscribed measures, but in reality do not have the possibility of influencing the transformation process of the city?

This happens, but it doesn't matter. The experience of the councils suggests that a utopian, extraordinary, idea is necessary, but to carry it out, very small steps must be taken, each of which must be a success. The small ones' proposals are collected in general because they are punctual, precise, concrete, and applicable. The small steps move towards a very distant goal. The two plans, the localized action and a very broad reference project, are easily settled and equally important. The small local action demonstrates to the young ones that a proposal can be fulfilled, and managed with public help, with their contribution, and that of their parents. In this way, the children do an exercise of citizenship that gives them the opportunity of believing that the greatest ideas can be realized.

In your opinion, what are the most significant consequences of these experiences?

If we exclude the children, one of the most important consequences concerns the stereotypical thinking of the adults. Parents, administrators, specialists, and teachers, discover with great astonishment that the small ones are totally different from the stereotypes of the dominant culture that considers them weak, incapable, dangerous and objects of inevitable control. The experience of the Councils calls into question this culture.

I think that another particularly significant aspect is the hope of a new relationship between the generations, which is rebuilt in terms of the future. ; this is especially important because, in a time of great decline in birth, the idea that adults are eternal has prevailed.

23. Other experiences: the educational cities

Interview with Fiorenzo Alfieri[84]

What is the Italian response to the project?

With regard to Italy, attempts are being made to relaunch and give greater meaning to the joining of our cities with the IAEC (International Association

---

[84] Fiorenzo Alfieri is director of the education system of the City Council of Turin.

of Educating Cities) which, meanwhile, has been established internationally and is under the observation of the UN and Unesco.

In January 1996, a large group of administrators met in Turin to discuss again the meaning of the "Charter", increase the number of participating cities, and organize the participation in Chicago. At this time, the idea of adopting the concept of "educating city" as a point of reference for socio-educational and cultural policies of cities with the same concept was being affirmed within the ANCI (National Association of Italian Municipalities) regarding childhood, young people, and family.

In Italy, the sensitive and cultural levels around these issues are very diverse. It is difficult to compare it with that of other countries. The feeling is that in some of our cities, very refined and advanced experiences are developed that can match those of other European countries. It seems to me that it can even be said that we are going through a good moment in the local administrations in regard to these issues. Also in the south, very motivated and creative administrators have entered the scene. The meetings between administrators are frequent and the multiplication of the most successful and feasible experiences should not be difficult. Above all, it seems to me that awareness is being generated that these issues have not only a specifically psycho-pedagogical value, but can be extrapolated to the primary interests of the community.

What perspectives can be pointed out for the future of the project?

An extraordinary, perhaps dramatic, need for education is being noticed. Regardless of the serious fact, on the other hand, that our country occupies the last place in Europe in the list of graduates and doctorates, there is no aspect of social life that does not state that, in addition to structural requirements, measures of an educational nature are a priority. When talking about defense of the environment, traffic, energy consumption, occupation, security, public order, solidarity, drug addiction, sex relations, maternity and paternity... the answer is always the same – it is not enough to offer manufactured goods and services, we must act on ways of thinking. We have to educate.

But who has this responsibility? And how is it put it into practice with some chance of success? If we seriously ask these questions, the affirmation of the educational priority, which already characterizes any position (of politicians and businessmen, of urban planners and economists), runs the risk of becoming a kind of background rumor without any effectiveness. The "Educating Cities" movement should become the optimal reference to answer these simple and now so compromising questions.

Interview with Pilar Figueras[85]

What is the International Association of Educating Cities and how did it start?

"Educating Cities" is a movement of cities represented by their local governments, which are grouped in order to work jointly and on several projects and activities that are proposed to all its inhabitants, from all areas and by different groups, with an educational drive.

This project was born as a result of the reflection of the mayor of Barcelona, Pascual Maragall, on the city; coinciding with the preparation of the Olympic Games. The Barcelona City Council proposed an international congress, in 1990, on the theme "The educating city, for children and young people". In this congress 70 cities participated from 21 countries that committed to comply with the principles of the Charter of Educating Cities. The conviction that the educating city needed to converse with other cities, reflect collectively, collaborate on projects... led the cities attending the international congress to create the International Association of Educating Cities (IAEC).

What are the objectives of this Association?

The Association basically intends to ensure compliance with the principles of the Charter of Educating Cities by the signatory cities – promote collaborations and concrete actions between cities, deepen the discourse of Educating Cities, and discuss and collaborate with the different national and international organizations. Since 1990 there has been an International Bank of Experiences of Educating Cities (IBEC).

What are the current contributions of Catalonia to this project?

The international congresses that are organized every two years serve, among other things, to extend the "Educating City" project around the city that organizes the congress.

For example, the congress organized in Barcelona served to give impetus to the project and, currently, an important part of the cities that make up the

---

[85] Pilar Figueras is the general secretary of the International Association of Educating Cities (IAEC), based in Barcelona.

"Educating Cities" movement are Spanish.[86] Since the statutes of the IAEC contemplate the possibility of the existence of territorial networks, a year ago the Spanish network was created in A Coruña, which is now coordinated by the city of Valencia, which was where the second meeting was held, in January 1998.

We are talking about territorial networks that promote exchanges about close realities. Creating thematic networks, more intersectional networks, where cities are grouped to work on common actions is also planned. In this, the International Bank of Experiences of Educating Cities (IBEC) plays a fundamental role, which is a valuable tool for consultation and exchange. It is a referential database that facilitates the knowledge of the educational offer of cities around the world, and promotes the exchange of experiences and the establishment of common concrete actions.

With regard to the area of Barcelona, the Barcelona Provincial Council prepares meetings and seminars aimed at concrete actions, but at the same time, it does very important work on the preparation of international congresses.

In addition, at the end of 1994, the mayor of Barcelona proposed the creation of an interdepartmental Commission within the City Council, so that all municipal areas made an offer of an educational sign on citizenship. This Commission should have several functions.

First, to make a certain "inventory" of the actions of educational content in the municipal area. It was expected that when this Commission had sufficient time to develop, another one, with a more citizen-based focus, would be created (with other cities, it has been started directly by the commissions of citizen focus).

Secondly, to see how these actions are understood by all citizens, since we are sure that certain groups of citizens are permanently uninformed. Thirdly, to analyze the degree of compliance with the principles of the Charter of Educating Cities, by the city of Barcelona. It would be a bit paradoxical to say that the Barcelona City Council, which inspires this entire movement, suggests and organizes the first congress, and proposes the Charter of

---

[86] Spanish cities part of IAEC: Alcobendas, Alcoi, Barcelona, Castellar del Vallès, Cerdanyola del Vallès, Cornellà de Llobregat, A Coruña, Gandía, Gijón, Girona, Granada, Granollers, Hospitalet de LLobregat, Lebrija, Lleida, Lugo, Málaga, Mataró , Palma de Mallorca, Pamplona, Pozuelo de Alarcón, Premià de Mar, Reus, Ripollet, Sabadell, Sant Boi de Llobregat, Sant Feliú de Guixols, Sant Joan Despí, Santa Coloma de Gramenet, Santa Cruz de Tenerife, Santiago de Compostela, Seville, Telde, Terrassa, Torrelavega, Valencia, Valladolid, Vigo, Viladecans.

Educating Cities, would not carefully analyze the degree to which its city has fulfilled its commitments.

Finally, this interdepartmental Commission has to consider what the contributions of the Barcelona City Council to the different international congresses will be. This is slow and long work since the demands of everyday life sometimes leave little room for new systematization of information.

What future challenges does the IAEC pose?

In principle, work to make the project "Educating City" a serious reality, with all of its utopian elements. All cities are educational, simply because they are cities, but educating cities are only those that show their willingness to be so.

This reality has two aspects: that of each city, and that which stimulates and facilitates being part of an international network within the framework of democracy and solidarity.

Work is also being carried out to prepare the next international congress, which will take place in Jerusalem in 1998, and which has been organized around the proposal "Know the past to project the future": to see what our city was, how it has reaffirmed our identity (culture, urban planning, services, health...) and, from here, build the future.

24. A national network that goes beyond

On December 17, 1994, the mayors of twenty cities met in Fano to learn about the experience of the Laboratory "The city of children" and evaluate the opportunity of taking this project to the municipalities themselves and promote a national network that allowed the coordination of the different experiences in motion on this subject. At the end of the day, the following document was approved:

The city has renounced its historical role of being a meeting point and place of exchange and has lost its citizens, having chosen, especially in recent decades, the strategies of separation and specialization, motivated almost exclusively by economic interest. Citizens have moved away from the city center, various areas have been created for different functions and categories: to sleep, to have fun, to buy, to heal, to study; for the elderly, for children, for the disabled, and so on.

The damage that has been caused to citizens has been compensated by means of services: transport, services for children, hypermarkets, public gardens, etc., to support an increasingly alienated life.

This agreement has been tacitly established between the administrators and the strong voters: the city has been designed and conceived adopting the average citizen as a parameter who, in general, has the characteristics of an adult, man and worker. In this way, the city has abandoned citizens who are not adults, not men and not workers.

The mayors propose: shifting the attention of the average citizen to the child; lowering the Administration's perspective to the child's level, so as not to lose any of the citizens it represents; learning to listen and understand the girls and boys, in their diversity, to be able to understand and represent all citizens.

It is not about defending the rights of a weak member of society among others. It is not about specifying initiatives, opportunities, and new structures for children; nor is it about modifying, updating, and improving services for children (which remains, however, a commitment of municipal administrations). Instead, it is about adopting a new philosophy when evaluating, programming, designing and modifying the city. A philosophy, of which the mayor becomes a guarantor and which becomes the soul of the municipal government program.

In particular, they are obliged to submit to their respective administrations the approval of a decree by means of which they acquire the following commitments:

1. To open in the city itself a Laboratory of "The city of girls and boys" that constitutes a point of connection and reference between the different directions and with the other interested cities.
2. Find the right formulas to directly include girls and boys in this project, both asking them to contribute ideas and offering them spaces to express their requirements and proposals to administrators.
3. Create a network of connection and confrontation between the cities joining the project that has the national organizational reference point for the dissemination of documents and information and for the organization of meetings in the Fano Laboratory.
4. Invite all other elected mayors to join this project in defense not only of children but also of all citizens and of the same cities.

This document, signed by the representatives of twenty-four cities and endorsed by the most important national associations, can also be signed and sent to the Fano Laboratory by the mayors who share it and intend to achieve its objectives.

Since 1994 the project has been spread in other municipalities, which have joined or are considering the possibility of putting it into practice.

The project was also presented in Spain and Argentina, where it managed to stimulate enormous interest among educators and authorities. In Argentina, the idea of organizing a national coordinator that links interested municipalities through Unicef Argentina and the Latin American Faculty of Social Sciences (FLacso) is being studied.

In order to respond to the growing interest shown by several cities, a research group was set up in 1996 at the Institute of Psychology of the CNR in Rome for the development of the project "The city of children", which would focus on:

- Deepening and developing the project through research and checking the experiences in operation.

- Extending the project to municipal administrations.

- Giving to the municipalities that want support at the beginning of, and in the development of, the project with a view of expanding the local competences.

- Documenting and publicizing the experiences underway.

Some of these functions may be absorbed by the institutional tasks of the Ministry of Environment and of Labor and Social Affairs.

To contact the research group, address to: International project "The city of children"

Institute of Cognition Sciences and Technologies of the National Research Council (CNR)

Via S. Martino della Battaglia, 44, 00185
Tel: +39 06 445 95205-445 295286
E-mail: *laboratorio@lacittadeibambini.org*
Web: *www.lacittadeibambini.org*

25. To start

Some advice and possible work proposals are listed below. Each city interested in the project can think of its own independent path. Here are some steps that were taken during the experience of Fano and in relation to the national network, developed in December 1994.

1. Verification from the mayor and the municipal government team that this project can and should become a new philosophy of the city government policy, taking into account that:

   - Currently, the citizens who also suffer from the harm of the city do not ask, at least explicitly, for a similar radical reform; therefore, a project like this does not constitute an obligation for administrators, only an option.

   - It is difficult to change a city in a way that responds to the needs and expectations of children because it is necessary to ask adults to give up some privileges that they probably already consider vested rights.

   - Once you join the project, you cannot betray it because it is a commitment made to children, and children cannot be lied to or mislead.

- It is a very important future option for the city, that responds to a deep need of the people, although not expressed, of maintaining hope for the future that cities are losing today.

2. Make the option public at a municipal plenary meeting, by joining the national network created in Rome by the CNR, making the active forces of the city (associations, schools, etc.) aware, and communicating it to the population with the initiatives that are considered appropriate.

3. Open a municipal Laboratory of "The city of children", providing it with personnel, premises and necessary means so that:

    - It constitutes a continuous stimulus to the rulers of the city for an increasingly coherent realization of the project.

    - It becomes a reference point for children and adults of the city about the city-children relationship.

    - It prepares a program of the initiatives to be taken.

    - It maintains contact with the Rome working group, providing materials that document the decisions and activities that are planned and carried out.

4. If the project is applied in a large city, it is necessary to identify a neighborhood or district in which specific activities can be carried out. It is important that the dimensions of the project application area are also "within the reach of the child". In the chosen area, a headquarters must be identified that becomes a reference point for the inhabitants, and a local work group must be employed to carry out the program. The Municipal Laboratory should make decentralized work possible and guarantee its documentation so that, as far as possible, it can be applied to larger areas of the city.

5. Encourage initiatives that tend to "give the floor to children", to allow them to contribute directly to the renovation of the city; already expressing their own opinions, and developing

attitudes of attention and listening in adults. Some possible activities:

- The Children's Council: the representatives (a boy and a girl) of the primary schools in the city or the neighborhood meet periodically in the premises of the Laboratory to discuss, with its members, the different proposals for the reform of the city; guaranteeing the children's perspective.

- Project-executing children: groups of children and young people who, within or outside of school, work together with city specialists (architects, urban planners, sociologists, psychologists, educators) to design urban spaces and services.

6. Convene a municipal plenary open to children at least once a year, during which there may be members of the Children's Council (see point 5) that have the floor to express proposals and protests; adults will have the duty to listen, understand, and give answers. It would be appropriate to dedicate a second meeting every year to the evaluation of the project and its future perspectives.

7. Cities that join the initiative can participate in organized national and international meetings, from which they will receive the appropriate information. They can also join the national and international campaigns, for example, the "My city and I" proposal that the city of Fano has been promoting for some years.

Appendix

1. Convention on the Rights of the Child*

Article 1: Everyone under 18 years of age has all the rights in this Convention.

Article 2: The Convention applies to everyone whatever their race, religion, abilities, whatever they think or say, whatever type of family they come from.

Article 3: The best interests of the child must be a top priority in all decisions and actions that affect children.

Article 5: Parents, or whoever responsible, should take care of the child.

Article 6:

1. Children have the right to live a full life.

2. States Parties shall ensure to the maximum extent possible the survival and development of the child.

Article 9: Children should not be separated from their parents, even if they are separated or divorced.

Article 10: Families who live in different countries should be allowed to move between those countries so that parents and children can stay in contact, or get back together as a family.

---

* This Convention on the Rights of the Child was approved by the United Nations on November 20, 1989 in New York. The Spanish government adopted it on January 26, 1990 and ratified it on December 6 of the same year. In the version that is published, the reader will appreciate that articles 4, 7-8, 25 and 36 have been omitted, as these are difficult for children to understand. In this sense, it has been simplified and reduced, by P. Benevene, F. Ippolito and F. Tonucci for the Basso Foundation (Italy). The simplified version of the English edition can be found also at: https://www.unicef.org.au/Upload/UNICEF/Media/Our%20work/childfriendlycrc.pdf or https://downloads.unicef.org.uk/wp-content/uploads/2010/05/UNCRC_summary-1.pdf?_ga=2.101325383.715187251.1569088442-250206478.1569088442

Article 11: Governments should take steps to stop children being taken out of their own country illegally.

Article 12: Children have the right to say what they think should happen when adults are making decisions that affect them and to have their opinions taken into account.

Article 13: Every child must be free to express their thoughts and opinions and to access all kinds of information, as long as it is within the law.

Article 14:

1. Children have the right to think and believe what they want and to practice their religion.

2. Parents should guide children on these matters.

Article 15: Children have the right to meet with other children.

Article 16: Children have the right to privacy.

Article 17: Mass media such as television, radio and newspapers should provide information that children can understand and should not promote materials that could harm children.

Article 18: If a child does not have any parents, someone should take care of it.

If the parents work, someone should take care of the child while they are at work.

Article 19: Governments should ensure that children are properly cared for and protect them from violence, abuse and neglect by their parents, or anyone else who looks after them.

Article 20: Children who cannot be looked after by their own family must be looked after properly by people who respect their religion, culture and language.

Article 21: The child has the right to be adopted if its family cannot take care of it. Business should not be made out of the adoption process.

Article 22:

1. If a child is seeking refuge or has refugee status, governments must provide them with appropriate protection and assistance to help them enjoy all the rights in the Convention.

2. Governments must help refugee children who are separated from their parents to be reunited with them.

Article 23:

1. Children who have a mental or physical disability have the right to live the same way other children live and by their side.

2. Children who have a mental or physical disability have the right to be cured.

3. Children who have a mental or physical disability have the right to go to school, prepare for work, have fun.

Article 24: Children have the right to good quality health care, clean water, nutritious food and a clean environment so that they will stay healthy. Richer countries should help poorer countries achieve this.

Article 26: Every child has the right to benefit from social security.

Article 27: Children have the right to a standard of living that is good enough to meet their physical and mental needs.

Article 28: Children have the right to an education. School should be free.

Article 29: Education must develop every child's personality, talents and abilities to the full. It must encourage the child's respect for human rights, as well as respect for their parents, their own and other cultures, and the environment.

Article 30: Children have the right to learn and use the language and customs of their families, whether or not these are shared by the majority of the people in the country where they live, as long as this does not harm others.

Article 31: Children have the right to relax, play and to join in a wide range of leisure activities.

Article 32: Governments should protect children from work that is dangerous or that might harm their health or education.

Article 33: Governments should provide ways of protecting children from dangerous drugs.

Article 34: Governments should protect children from sexual abuse.

Article 35: Governments should make sure that children are not abducted or sold.

Article 37: Children must not be tortured, sentenced to the death penalty or suffer other cruel or degrading treatment or punishment. Children should be arrested, detained or imprisoned only as a last resort and for the shortest time possible. They must be treated with respect and care, and be able to keep in contact with their family.

Article 38: Governments should not allow children under 15 to join the army. Children in war zones should receive special protection.

Article 39: Children who have been neglected or abused should receive special help to restore their self-respect.

Article 40: A child accused or guilty of breaking the law must be treated with dignity and respect. They have the right to legal assistance and a fair trial that takes account of their age.

Article 41: If the laws of a particular country protect children better than the articles of the Convention, then those laws should override the Convention.

Article 42: Governments should make the Convention known to all parents and children.

2. A call to collaborate: an open letter to the citizens of Fano

Fano's City Council has established "Fano the city of children", a regional Laboratory for planning and experimenting with proposals that improve the difficult relationship that exists today between the city and the child.

Children often live alone, they cannot meet spontaneously to play, they have no space or time of their own, the streets are occupied by cars, the city is dangerous.

Working to make the city fit for children means working to make the city more suitable for everyone.

We plan to invite the administrators of other cities to Fano to discuss these problems with each other, and between ourselves; we plan to invite the children from other cities to Fano to offer them our friendship, our ideas. We would like Fano to become the point of reference for this delicate issue.

But if the city must change, the change cannot be entrusted or delegated solely to the Administration. The widespread delegation and the welfare attitude derived from it have probably been the cause of the deterioration of our cities. For the city to change, everyone can and should do something.

This letter is a personal invitation for all those who have an active role in the various productive, service or cultural sectors of our city to ask the question: "What can I do for the children of my city?"; "What can I invent so that the child can benefit from my knowledge?"; "What opportunities can I propose or suggest?".

There is room for creativity. Moreover, we are convinced that only by inventing new things can we trust in achieving something good. A factory, a museum, an office, a craft workshop, a shop, a station, a boat... no doubt hide something – an initiative, an itinerary that can interest a child or can improve its life as a young citizen.

If everyone does something, even if only thinking a little, and even if nothing much comes to mind, Fano will begin to change.

You can go to the headquarters of the Laboratory to propose, offer, request clarifications or collaboration.

On behalf of the children and the working group, we thank you for your attention and hope to see you again in the Laboratory.

Fano, December 1991

Director of the Laboratory   The mayor of Fano
Francesco Tonucci   *Francesco Baldarelli*

3. Lewis Mumford, "Planning for the different stages of life"*

Almost a generation ago, in a copy of *Survey Graphic* (May 1925), Dr. Hart pointed out the fact that urban planning was conceived in terms of a particular stage of life – that of adults free of family responsibilities. He highlighted the meaning of the old saying that 'the people of the boulevards never grow old'; that the boulevard, because of its function and its structure, always attracts groups of the same age, who move for the same interests and pursue the same goals.

Despite this warning, the urban planner has not yet fully realized his key function, which is to provide an environment suitable for any stage of life, from childhood to senility.

Urban activity has so far concentrated almost exclusively on the lives of adults and usually only on certain aspects of their lives, such as business, industry, administration, traffic, and transport.

Even when taking care of adults, urban planning omits important areas of activity. The purpose of this study is to briefly explore the field that Dr. Hart opened. Keeping in mind the various stages of life, urban planners may modify their attitude to both the method and the purpose of planning. In this case, perhaps this would lead to the revision of the projects of certain groups, such as play areas, where administrative comfort has led to the repetition of certain schemes whose external order reflects an inner sterility. If the awareness of the cycle of human life serves as nothing else, it could at least be useful as a checklist of needs, to discover the weaknesses in a seemingly admirable plan.

First stage: childhood

It's about seeing what planning can do for the child from birth to the age of going to school. Above all, the question of housing is planned: in fact, while in all countries, during the last generation, there has been a decided orientation towards births in hospitals, now it is suspected that this is not the best condition for a normal delivery, or for the first days of the newborn's life. The experiences of numerous health centers seem to indicate the advantages of home delivery, especially from a psychological point of view. However, even there, where the living conditions are the most suitable, childbirth leads to a disruption in the usual rhythm of the house and causes a transitory disorder.

The urban planner should find an intermediate solution between the expensive hospital, provided with the necessary installations in case of

---

* Published in the magazine *Urbanística*, No. 1 (1945).

emergency, and the house that does not offer the necessary space for the child's birth. The solution could be a small neighborhood clinic, which would be an integral part of a complex of 250-500 families, perhaps dependent on a local hospital so that the possibilities of the latter could be available. In this way, the mother could be close to her other children, easily receive visits from her husband, and be assisted by her relatives. This solution would restore the human element, which is being lost in those that have been defined as "disease warehouses".

With regard to childhood, planning the greatest care should be taken to ensure that the mother finds peace and rest, free from the daily pressure of domestic duties. The absence of tension is, in effect, the best condition for creating a serene and affectionate relationship between a mother and child. But, on the other hand, the organization should under no circumstances be a closed unit in itself; neighbors are needed not only in emergencies, but also in daily life.

Even in the most extensive housing areas, where there are thirty families per hectare, there is usually an absence of a meeting place for mothers and children, where they can work while chatting and without losing sight of their children playing. Perhaps the best part of Charles Reilly's plan for garden cities was the one that predicted such activity, as the designers of Sunnyside, Stein and Wright, have done since 1924.

In this order of ideas, planning must find appropriate, warm, and protective solutions. Children, up to approximately ten years of age, need limited spaces – hiding places – and the walls, hedges, caves, and holes can meet these needs.

Children under six must feel the connection with their environment, must have sand, pebbles, stones and branches for their games and, to prevent them from becoming young vandals, the most basic type of playing field should be installed in a sandy, dry hollow, surrounded by a cobbled path, around which mothers can sit and watch. This area should be away from the rest of the enclosure separated by a wall and a fence, which children cannot pass, and in the center there should be a large stone or, better yet, caves and hiding places.

Those who love gardens generally tend to deprive children of the freedom they need to dig and make their constructions. On the other hand, if the children's games were made collective and the mothers were brought together, the children would be given greater freedom and would be prepared for other forms of cooperation.

Second stage: school years

The path from home to school is a critical moment for the child. The shock and psychological trauma of not only the loss of the mother's protective vigilance, but also the diversity in the scale and proportion of the building compared to their private home which is often a gigantic complex of constructions, terrifying in its impersonal immensity, is often underestimated. In some large cities, such as San Francisco, elementary schools are still relatively small and in the most modern schools, classes have their own play area that is not incorporated into the structure of the building.

Perhaps the best way to complete the transition is to have an elementary school in the neighborhood itself. There, mothers trained to provide assistance in surveillance would be employed rather than specialized personnel. Although planning cannot anticipate new social organizations, it is capable, depending on the occasion, of suggesting them and indicating the most appropriate one. It seems that in Zurich, this collaboration has been achieved by mothers in some kindergartens.

The child's walk from home to school should be fun and educational without it realizing.

Sometimes the child knows how to extract unsuspected treasures from a pile of garbage and a puddle can become a lake; but where the division into zones is too rigid and the suburban residential area is relentlessly tidy and clean, there is no longer any relief for its imagination.

In order for a child to truly grasp the meaning of the world in which it lives, it would be necessary for the daily walk to be in direct contact with nature, such as in rural areas, or with the work of people in factories or markets. The activities that serve a neighborhood should not be segregated too much and the child could have some small errands and purchases among its tasks. This need is felt less in Europe than in America, where the norms of the respectability of the middle classes and the use of cars have created an extreme separation between commercial and residential areas.

In our effort to provide the necessary space for children's games, we have often forgotten the fascination of spontaneous play in their lives, especially within new communities. In the asphalted fields, the child's fantasy disappears, while, for example, wonderful possibilities arise in the bombed areas of London. The author recalls from his own youth the open fields, on the outskirts of New York, with rocky surfaces where apples and potatoes were roasted. Hedges could be used to hide out of sight, those places that should remain rather messy, which must be the urban equivalent of those wild places that children like so much. The best contribution to these areas would be to build them in a hollow, to artificially create the possibilities of adventure.

Third stage: adolescence

With adolescence, the neighborhood is no longer the only center of activity for the young. In secondary school, there are children from other locations, organized games are held, they do not travel to and from the city alone, but they walk around.

At some point in our civilization, the idea that has matured in the minds of philosophers and educators, from Fourier to Goethe and from Schreber to William James, the idea of the army of labor, will eventually find a place in our educational system. It will not be easy to accept it, but the best system will be practice; and just as there are parents who have a sense of family responsibility only after being entrusted with children, good citizens will be created by entrusting young people with some activities in the community. The best way to begin the constructive function of the army of labor will be the care and maintenance of common goods.

If we can allow for parks, wooded areas and gardens, which we foresee in the new type of open planning, we will be prohibited by the maintenance costs unless we make it a civil service; voluntary if possible, mandatory if necessary. The maintenance of open areas, the care of plants and flowers could be the role of future generations of adolescents – one of the many moral equivalents of a war, which a pacifist generation must face.

Somehow this would be a preparatory role, because the beneficiaries would be the young people themselves in the next stage of their life – that of their first romantic relationships. The period of late adolescence, when sexual energies are imperative and there is relatively not much relief, is a difficult and dangerous time for boys and girls. It is often a time of inner conflict, whose commotion should be balanced by the contemplation of the surrounding beauty. If prolonging childhood has been the first sign of the evolution of man, prolonging the sentimental period with its visible results in art, music, literature and religion represents an even more advanced stage. This elaboration of the erotic impulses intensifies it, but giving meaning and sentiment to the purely instinctive manifestations. In the countryside, couples have no difficulty in finding the secluded places appropriate for their mood, but in our cities, courtship becomes too short or furtive, oppressed and difficult, exasperating.

The Labyrinth, the favorite theme of the baroque urban planners, is undoubtedly a means to that end. F. Law Olmsted, when designing the Central Park of New York, built the Ramble (the "promenade"), which, with its irregular topography, is a place where we can get lost, with the admirable result that this is perhaps the only place in New York that lends itself to romantic recreation.

If urban planners had the different stages of life in mind, they would not be so insensitive to the needs of the final stage of adolescence that wants places of solitary beauty that accentuate and expand, even by cooling down their impulses, and enrich them with visual images that feed their happy mood.

Fourth stage: Maturity

The work stage

Along with the growing division of labor in modern times, another process occurs – the intensification and segregation of labor. Both the peasant and the artisan, at other times, worked for a much longer number of hours than modern workers, but their work was spent in an environment that had other aspects and customs – it was carried out in the family environment, often with the collaboration of all its members. There were no walls, visual or functional, between work, the domestic environment, and education. The era of specialization, focusing solely on mechanical efficiency, has deprived work life of some of its aesthetic and human dimensions. Alsoin this field, in modern cities, we will have to try to bring these diverse aspects of life together again, which, separated, almost automatically creates divisions and disharmonies in personality.

Nor in this case, however, will it be possible to return to the primitive forms. New forms will have to be found as far from the artisan laboratory as from the terrible Victorian factories.

The authors of *Communitas* propose that homes and factories be built around urban squares. According to the description made by Philip and Percival Goodman, it seems that in this way an archaic model of close association would be formed voluntarily, while what it is actually about is finding and appropriate modern model.

The authors propose that the social and domestic functions of the working days be introduced in industrial areas, both in the renewed and in the newly created ones: for example, accessible play areas at meal times or during other intervals; different dining rooms, instead of the common dining room; meeting rooms for committees, available not only to an area but to the entire unit, to carry out the political relations of managers or workers; school buildings and museums.

In some industrial establishments these functions have been incorporated into the industrial structure – it is now necessary to organize entire industrial districts on the basis of the same principles, with even more advanced functional and spatial ideas.

The same principle applies to neighborhoods of commercial activity. While in North America the first sign of "progress" in a city is to tear down the trees on the main street, in Paris the great contribution of Hausmann in creating the new boulevards was to make the activities of business, recreation and of social relations possible; perhaps nowhere else in the center of Paris have the various activities of the adult been so closely grouped. The segregation of duties, practiced with the sole interest of mechanical efficiency, does not produce an interesting social life or fully developed personality.

The domestic stage

When a young couple has a house with a small garden located among thousands of other similar houses, society thinks that it has achieved the best for family life, and in fact, it is already a lot. When such a house can be had without absorbing too much of the annual income, a great step is taken towards the rehabilitation of family life. In this sense, considerations could be made about the family life of the middle classes in the Victorian period, when all the comforts that could be had in the intimacy of the family meant that its members felt no desire to spend time away from home that was not strictly necessary for work. But this family intimacy would not be enough either, because the family would be prone to isolation, absorbed in itself, hostile to the subsequent development of its members. That is why something else is necessary for the success of family life – sociability and interests beyond the home, first by the spouses and then, within the limits of their possibilities, also by the younger members of the family. In this case, the inventiveness of the urban planner must be sharpened to find a way to achieve, in social and economic life, what surrounded the bourgeois family life of three generations ago in the private one.

The Peckham Health Center has, among other things, the advantage of offering families of the area the possibility of meeting places outside the domestic confines, where groups of different ages, now separated by the diversity and intensity of individual interests, can come together again or at least frequent work and entertainment, without being out of sight of other family members.

Precisely the fact of "not being out of sight" is one of the attributes that tend to unite communities and that have often been neglected in modern planning. Perhaps the most rudimentary definition of a community is this: a grouping of people who live without losing sight of each other. Even in a secluded area, being able to see a light in the neighbor's house gives a sense of security and sociability. It is not advisable at all that parents are their children's constant companions, but relationships will be better if each one has an idea of what the other is doing, rather than their respective activities being so disconnected as if they lived in different worlds.

In response to the terrible state of chaos and spatial disorganization, modern planners have reached a uniformity based on dispersion, which can undermine the social sense as much as excessive congestion does. In this sense, it can be said that a shopping center, similar to the medieval market squares, and in contrast to the endless streets with scattered shops, concentrates and multiplies the chances of meetings, exchanges and greetings; that is to say, the minimum social activities that tend to renew good neighborhood and friendly relationships.

It is better to risk a bit of crowding in a restricted area than to plan a center so spacious that it can comfortably contain the maximum conceivable load, with the result of making it socially cold on normal occasions and impractical due to the loss of time that it would cause.

The Settlement House, community centers and health centers are not inconsiderable attempts to create focal points for specific activities outside the domestic environment.

In North America, there is now a tendency to place meeting places for non-domestic activities in the neighborhood schools, because most of these adult activities take place in the hours when the school is closed. Therefore, the use of auditoriums, swimming pools, laboratories, etc., is not exclusive to schools only; with the condition that the facilities are left so as the students can use them. But adults need an even simpler form of meeting place – a place capable of accommodating about fifty seated people, where discussions and eventual parties, for which the private house is too small, can take place. One of the happiest ideas in Patrik Geddes' report on Dunfermline is to reserve a beautiful historic house that can be temporarily rented to those families who want to use it for receptions and large gatherings. In a community of five thousand people, it would take at least five rooms with a kitchen and bathrooms.

The base of the social relationships

This stage should properly be called civic, understanding with this term the willingness to live together in a city.

A city that fully develops its function represents the life of the entire world and thus contains a variety of products, people, organizations, associations and beliefs that are not commonly found in other specialized communities. While similarities and affinities are emphasized in the town (and the same is true in the city's neighborhoods), the city must emphasize and reconcile the varieties, differences and antagonisms. Good planning will multiply the occasions to amalgamate and merge the various trends.

Today, two forces stop the reciprocal attraction of citizens as such: one is made up of fast means of transport, radio and other mechanical inventions, which tend to scatter community members in increasingly vast areas; the other is the tendency of segregation, which is especially felt in large urban agglomerations and is accentuated by the progressive division into zones. A function that, at least in the United States, often separates classes and groups according to their respective income and race into clearly identifiable neighborhoods; so that there is no relationship between the "upper strata" and "lower strata." Thus, each group, or class, or caste, lives in a world that denies the multiple cooperation of all human communities in the social architectural organization. In the United States, suburban expansion tends toward such an extension of proportions that, despite the large presence of vehicles, life in common has become increasingly difficult, resulting in social isolation that increases in proportion according to the area and the population.

Planning for the various stages of life

From the point of view of relations between citizens, the task of planning must be to maximize the resources of positive and negative cooperation. A good square will multiply the chances of accidental and unforeseen encounters, as they occur in a market or in public places of eating and drinking. The Welwyn City warehouse, for example, is already on a disproportionate scale with the community, but with its large dining room, it offers an indispensable focal point for community life. According to these concepts, the planner will multiply the internal spaces of the city, where the public can meet for various purposes.

A square that does not have the purpose of promoting the daily union of people, classes, and activities, works against the best interests of the middle-aged.

The individual stage

This analysis demonstrates the need to develop certain public activities that have already been carried out privately by cautious and protective people – that is, the intention is to distribute these activities throughout the community. Emerson had already raised the problem of the public transformation of certain personal prerogatives when he declared he needed books, but did not want to become a bookseller, and that he liked paintings without wanting to become a museum curator. The rule applies both to functions that must be socialized and to those that must be de-socialized, for example, loneliness. One of the signs of maturity is the need for solitude and the city must not only bring people together, but must also allow everyone to have at their fingertips the places necessary for isolation and peace. The function of the spiritual retreat is no longer what the medieval cloister required, but must be considered a daily necessity. The fascination of the Westminster neighborhood lies in its maze of alleyways where the lone walker can get lost a short distance from the most hectic center. In the new communities, on a smaller scale and with a lower density, the art of achieving the same results must be acquired. In the parks that connect the neighborhoods, for example, there can be wider streets outside, while the interior area will be lined with paths, so that crossing the boundaries from the community to find solitary places to spend a few minutes or a few hours is not necessary. A considerable part of our ideas for architectural and urban planning has so far been directed to external activities, which is great for social and public relations, but destructive for moments of recollection, spiritual intimacy and solitude. These must be supported by the environment, for which spaces and possibilities must be provided in the project of a collective plan of the city.

Final stage: senility

Perhaps no phase of life has been so neglected in our civilization, and also by urbanism, as old age.

In the western world, for half a century, the family of three generations has been reduced to two. A sign of this evolution is the increase in the number of separate family groups, even when the proportion of births is decidedly in decline. But, while the number of elderly people increases in each country thanks to the progress of hygiene and medical care, there is no notable effort in regard to their arrangements. Pensions are not sufficient compensation for their increasing social relegation. In small homes, the presence of the elderly is unwanted even in the best cases, in such a way that the prolongation of their existence becomes a bitter irony, because it progressively finds itself reduced and deprived of meaning.

In the harmonious reconstruction of family life, which is one of the purposes of urban planning, one of the main objectives will be to give the elderly a dignified and fruitful position.

If it is not possible to recover the family of three generations, it will be necessary to find the means to form a community of three generations – the mixture of different age groups is essential for a balanced life, as well as the mixture of social and economic classes.

There are many important social functions that the elderly can perform as long as their mental faculties have not been reduced. Women can participate in housekeeping. The elderly, although often their status does not allow them to earn the salary of a full day's work, can still be excellent gardeners, make repairs, guard and watch.

The community should not be considered as well planned if it does not contribute to a particular organization of the elderly, precisely because of the great utility that can be obtained from them. A small housing unit on one floor, not segregated from the rest of the dwellings and which can accommodate a few couples or several individuals, will be an excellent measure for the elderly as long as they do not need the continuous care and surveillance of a residence.

These units should be located near schools, markets or playgrounds, because the elderly need the reassurance of active life to overcome their loneliness and the growing feeling of alienation and humiliation that age brings.

The homes of the elderly citizens should always be on the ground floor, not overlooking internal courtyards, but with a view of what is happening on the exterior to make their life interesting. The different groups of elders should settle close enough to their families to maintain contact and be able to give their help in vigilance and assistance, participating, without having the feeling of being a useless burden, in the lives of their children or their neighbors.

The only admissible project in the care and organization of the elderly will be the one that avoids their segregation and institutionalization. Also, in this case, the principle of having them "within reach" and "not losing sight of them" will be the most important to reestablish the foundations of these small intimacies, adventures, and stimuli; that the neighborhoods of more comfortable housing, if they are too segregated or too large, cannot offer.

An organic conception of urban planning, which encompasses all stages of life as much as the functions of the community, should suggest solutions so far ignored by a more technical and specialized point of view.

When recovering the balance within the citizen community, one must think about restoring the equilibrium over time by means of reciprocal relations between the different stages of life, because each step of our existence has its particular requirements that can be satisfied only when the coordinated needs of other age groups are taken into consideration.

What is essential when formulating a guideline for a project on these bases is the return to the human scale – to the most accessible dimension units, to an order visible to the naked eye, to a conception of the community, which is not a maze of large collective organizations, but a constantly variable combination of a multitude of associative activities, varying in intensity and duration, and in continuous development throughout the life cycle, from birth to death.

Bibliography

A better life in the urban environment

ASCHER, F. (1991): «The future of the cities», *Architecture & Comportement*, 7 (4), pp. 323-339.

BISQUERT, A. (1982): *El niño y la ciudad*, Madrid, Colegio Oficial de Arquitectos de Madrid.

CERVELLATI, P. L. (1991): *La città bella*, Bolonia, Il Mulino.

GANDINO, B. and MANUETTI, D. (1990): *La città possibile: Manuale per rendere più vivibile e accogliente l´ambiente urbano*, Como, Red Edizioni.

GEHL, J. (1991): *Vita in città*, Rímini, Maggioli.

KROLL, L. (1991): «L'urbanisme fragmenté», *Architecture & Comportement*, 7 (2), pp. 193-197.

MEAD, M. (1996): «Neighborhoods and Human Need», *Ekistics*.

PIRODDI, E. and COLAROSSI, P. (1991): «Le projet urbain: De la fragmentation à la recomposition», *Architecture & Comportement*, 7 (4), pp. 357-367.

REBOIS, D. (1991): «Fragmentations et articulations urbaines», *Architecture & Comportement*, 7 (4), pp. 305-306.

URBANISMO Y MUJER. NUEVAS VISIONES DEL ESPACIO PÚBLICO Y PRIVADO (Actas del Curso, Málaga, 1993; Toledo, 1994): *Ciudad y mujer*, Madrid, Seminario permanente ciudad y mujer, 1995.

WEBER, F. and WEBER, J. (1989): «La ville de demain», *Architecture & Comportement*, 5 (1), pp. 68-70.

The child and the urban environment

AA.VV. (1992 a): I confini della città, Florencia, Centro di Documentazione Michelucci, nº 1.

— 1992 b «Bambini e bambine: Qualità dell'ambiente urbano», *Albero ad elica*, nº 2, Cosenza.

— 1994 «La condizione dei bambini nella metropoli diffusa», *LiBeR*, nº 22, Región Toscana, Comune Campo di Bisenzio.

ALEXANDER, C. et al. (1980): *A pattern language*, New York, Oxford University Press, 1977. Edición española: *Un lenguaje de palabras*, Barcelona, Gustavo Gili.

ALTMANN, I. and WOHLWILL, J. F. (editors) (1978): *Human Behavior and environment, 3, Children and the environment*, New York, Plenum Press.

AMENDOLA, G. (1995): «Il bambino invisibile e la città immaginaria», *Paessagio urbano*, 2, pp. 11-16.

BALDESCHI, P. (1995): «La città dei bambini è la città di tutti», *Paessagio urbano*, 2, pp. 5-10.

BASSAND, M. (1995): «L'enfant et la dynamique urbain: approche sociologique», *Architecture & Comportement*, 11 (1), pp. 43-54.

CHAWLA, L. (1995): «Revisioning childhood, nature, and city», *Architecture & Comportement*, 11 (1), pp. 11-18.

CHOMBART DE LAUWE, M. J. (1980): «L'ambiente urbano fonte di difficoltà per il bambino?», en AA.VV., *Il bambino e la città*, Milán, Franco Angeli, pp. 113-128.

COHEN, M. I. (1979): «The urban adolescent's interfaces with his environment: Health and meaningful survival», in MICHELSON, W.; LEVINE, S. V. and MICHELSON, E. (editors): *The child in the city: Today and tomorrow*, Toronto, University of Toronto Press, pp. 193-205.

COULOMB, A. (1995): «L'enfant, la ville, quel quotidien?», *Architecture & Comportement*, 11 (1), pp. 72-77.

GERMANOS, D. (1995): «La relation de l'enfant a l'espace urbain: perspectives educatives et culturelles», *Architecture & Comportement*, 11 (1), pp. 54-63.

GRUSSU, S. and PAGLIARINI, C. (1987): *Ragazzi di città*, Teramo, Giunti & Lisciani Editori.

KRANTZ, B. and RASMUSSON, B. (1995): «Changing perspectives and approaches: Swedish research on children and the urban environement», *Architecture & Comportement*, 11 (1), pp. 27-34.

LORENZO, R. (1993): «A scuola, in strada, in città: il bambino urbano in città», *Edilizia scolastica*, n° 2, Florencia.

LYNCH, K. (1979): «Growing up in cities», text from a presentation in Montreal, Mit Archives, compil. pp. 89-115, b. 1.

MUMFORD, L. (1945): «La pianificazione per le diverse fasi della vita», *Urbanística*, 1, pp. 711.

NORDSTROM, M. (1995): «Childhood Environmental Memories. What are they and to what use do we put them?», *Architecture & Comportement*, 11 (1), pp. 19-26.

NOSCHIS, K. (1992): «L'enfant intérieur et la ville», *Architecture & Comportement*, 8 (1), pp. 49-59.

— 1994 «The urban child», *Architecture & Comportement*, 10 (4), pp. 351-360.

PASSOV, C. K. (1980): «Aspetti positivi e negativi dell'influenza della città sui bambini», in AA. VV., *Il bambino e la città*, Milán, Franco Angeli, pp. 196-216.

PARR, A. E. (1967): «The child in the city: Urbanity and urban scene», *Landscape*.

PENNARTZ, P. J. and ELSINGA, M. J. (1990): «Adults, adolescents, and architects. Differences in perception of the urban environment», *Environment and Behavior*, 22 (5), pp. 675-714.

SAITA, L. and SUFFINI, G. et al. (1993): *Modena: la città delle bambine e dei bambini*, Modena, Comune di Modena.

SPENCER, C. (1995): «The child's environment: A challenge for psychologist and planner alike», in D. Canter (editor): *The child's environment*, London, Harcourt Brace & Company Publisher.

TONUCCI, F. (1994): *La soledad del niño*, Barcelona, Barcanova.

WARD, C. (1976): *The child in the city*, London, Architecture Press.

— 1980 «I bambini e l'ambiente urbano di città», in AA.VV.: *Il bambino e la città*, Milán, Franco Angeli, pp. 243-251.

Perceptual and cognitive aspects of the urban environment

AXIA, G. (1986): *La mente ecológica, conoscenza dell'ambiente nel bambino*, Florencia, Giunti Barbera.

BONNES, M. and RULLO, G. (1995): «Percezioni, immagini, mappe mentali della città nei bambini», *Paessagio urbano*, 2, pp. 26-29.

CHAWLA, L. (1992): «Childhood place attachment, human behavior and environment», in ALTMAN, I. and LOW, S. M. (editors): *Human behavior and environment. Advances in theory and research*, New York, Plenum Press, pp. 63-96.

GASTER, S. (1995): «Rethinking the children's homerange concept», *Architecture & Comportement*, 11 (1), pp. 34-41.

HART, R (1979): *Children's experience of place*, New York, Irvington.

LIBEN, L. S. (1991): «Environmental cognition through direct and representional experiences: A life span perspective», in GARLING, G. and EVANS, G. W. (editors): *Environment, cognition, and action: An Integrate approach*, New York, Oxford University Press, pp. 245-276.

LYNCH, K. (1966): *L'immagine della città*, Venecia, Marsilio Editori, 1960. Edición española: *La imagen de la ciudad*, Buenos Aires, Ediciones In- finito.

LYNCH, K. (1979): «The spatial world of the child», in MICHELSON, W.; LEVINE, S. V. and MICHELSON, E. (editors): *The child in the city: Today and tomorrow*, Toronto, University of Toronto Press. Spanish edition: LYNCH, K.: *La buena forma de la ciudad*, Barcelona, Gustavo Gili.

MORALES, M. (1984): *El niño y el medio ambiente. Orientaciones y actividades para la primera infancia*, Barcelona, OikosTau.

MORALES, M.; VENTALLÓ, E. and TONUCCI, F. (1996): *Barcelona amb ulls de nen*, Barcelona, P. A. U.

MUNTAÑOLA, J. (1983): *El nen i l'entorn. Orientacions per als infants de 7 a 10 anys*, Barcelona, OikosTau.

— 1996 *La arquitectura como lugar*, Barcelona, Edicions U. P. C.

MUNTAÑOLA, J. and DOMÍNGUEZ, J. (1992): *Barcelona avaluada pels seus infants*, Barcelona, Ajuntament de Barcelona.

PERON, E. M. and FALCHERO, S. (1994): *Ambienti e conoscenza: aspetti cognitivi della psicologia ambientale*, Roma, La Nuova Italia Scientifica.

PROSHANSKY, H. M. and FABIAN, A. K. (1987): «The development of place identity in the city», in WEINSTEIN, C. S. T. and DAVID, G. (editors): *Space for children: The built environment and child development*, New York, Plenum Press, pp. 21-39.

SKANTZE, A. (1995): «Experiencing and interpreting city architecture», *Architecture & Comportement*, 11 (1), pp. 5-10.

SPENCER, C. (1991): «Lifespan changes in activities and consequent changes in the cognition and assessment of the environment», in GAR LING, T. and EVANS, G. W. (editors): *Environment, cognition and action: An integrate approach*, New York, Oxford University Press, pp. 295-309.

TSOUKALA, K. (1995): «La ville en tant qu'environment d'expériences pour l'enfant», *Architecture & Comportement*, 11 (1), pp. 63-68.

The playing in the urban environment

ADER, J. and JOUVE, H. (1991): «Jeu et contexte urbain», *Architecture & Comportement*, 7 (2), pp. 115-119.

BOZZO, L.: «Il gioco e la città», *Paesaggio urbano*, 2, 1995, pp. 3033.

BROUGÈRE, G. (1991): «Espace de jeu et espace public», *Architecture & Comportement*, 7 (2), pp. 165-177.

CARBONARAMOSCATI, V. (1985): «Barriers to play activities in the city environment: A study of children's perception», in GARLING, T. and VALSINER, J. (editors): *Children within environment: Toward a psychology of accident prevention*, New York, Plenum Press, pp. 119-126.

DANACHER, A. (1991): «Contraintes de l'espace ludique aménagé», *Architecture & Comportement*, 7 (2), pp. 153-165.

GOLTSMAN, S. (1992): *Play for all: Planning, design, and management of outdoor play settings for all children*, Berkeley, MIG Comunication.

GUICHARD, S. and ADER, J. (1991): «La ville à jouer», *Architecture & Comportement*, 7 (2), pp. 123-137.

KROLL, L. (1990): «Vers la ruejeu, par une reconquête des espaces publics», *Architecture & Comportement*, 7 (2), pp. 177-192.

LADD, F. C. (1977): «City kids in the absence of legitimate adventure», text from a presentation in Upper Darby, Pennsylvania.

LECCESE, M. (1995): «Per una nuova definizione del concetto di gioco», *Paesaggio urbano*, 2, pp. 51-53.

MARILLAUD, J. (1991): «Jeu et securité dans l'espace public», *Architecture & Comportement*, 7 (2), pp. 137-145.

The mobility of the child in the urban environment

ANDREWS, H. F. (1973): «Home range and urban knowledge of school age children», *Environment & Behavior*, 5, pp. 73-84.

BERTOLINI, P. and CARDARELLO, R. (1989): *Da casa a scuola: gli indicatori soggettivi della qualità della vita infantile*, Florencia, La Nuova Italia Scientifica.

BJORKLID, P. (1985): «Children's outdoor environment from the perspective of environmental and developmental psychology», in GARLING, T. and VALSINER, J. (editors): *Children within environment: Toward a psychology of accident prevention*, New York, Plenum Press, pp. 91-105.

BJORKLID, P. (1994): «Children traffic environment», *Architecture & Comportement*, 10 (4), pp. 361-369.

BONANOMI, L. (1994): «L'enfant et la traversée de la chaussée», *Architecture & Comportement*, 10 (4), pp. 399-406.

GARLING, T., SVENSSONGARLING, A. and VALSINER, J. (1984): «Parental concern about children's traffic safety in residential neighborhoods», *Journal of Environmental Psychology*, 4, pp. 235-352.

GARLING, T.; SVENSSONGARLING, A.; MAURITZONSANDBERG, E. and BJORNSTING, U. (1989): «Children safety in the home: mother's perception of dangers to young child», *Architecture & Comportement*, 5 (4), pp. 239-305.

GASTER, S. (1991): «Urban children's access to neighborhood», *Environment & Behavior*, 23 (1), pp. 70-85.

HILLMAN, M. (1993): «Children transport and quality of life», *Policy Studies Institute*, London.

HILLMAN, M.; ADAMANS, J. and WHITELEGGI, J. (1990): «One false move: A study of children's independent mobility», *Policy Studies Institute*, London.

LEE, T. and ROWE, N. (1994): «Parent's and children's perceived risk of the journey to school», *Architecture & Comportement*, 10 (4), pp. 379-389.

PARR, E. A. (1967): «The child in the city: Urbanity and the urban scene», *Landscape*, spring.

POAG, C. K.; GOODNIGHT, J. A. and COHEN, R. (1985): «The environment of children, from home to school», in Cohen, R. (editor): *The development of spatial cognition*, New Jersey, Lawrence Erlbaum, Hillsdale, pp. 71-113.

SANDELS, S. (1975): *Children in traffic*, London, Elek Books.

TORREL, G. and BIEL, A. (1985): «Parental restriction and children's acquisition of neighborhood knowledge», in GARLING, T. and VALSINER, J. (editors): *Children within environment: Toward of psychology of accident prevention*, New York, Plenum Press, pp. 107-117.

Children and shared planning

BISHOP, J. (1995): «Bambini disegnatori e progettisti», *Paesaggio urbano*, 2, pp. 54-59.

DRUM, M. (1994): «Abitare urbano», texto de la ponencia en al Seminario *La città in tasca: Dalla progettazione partecipata alla qualità deglo spazi urbani*, Caserta.

DRUM, M. (1995): «Monaco: l'esperienza di Urbanes Wohnen per la riqualificazione degli spazi urbani», *Paesaggio urbano*, 2, pp. 64-77.

FRANCIS, M. (1993): «Negotiating between child and adult design values», *Design Studies*, 9 (2), pp. 67-75.

— 1995 «Il luogo per un'infanzia naturalistica», *Paesaggio urbano*, 2, pp. 44-50.

HART, R. (1987): «Children's participation in planning and design: Theory, research and practice», in Weisten, C. S. and David, T. G. (editors): *Space for children: The built environment and child development*, New York, Plenum Press.

— 1991 «Developmental perspectives on decision making and action in environments», in GARLING, G. and EVANS, G. W. (editors): *Environment, cognition, and action: An integrate approach*, New York, Oxford University Press, pp. 277-294.

— 1992 «Children's participation from tokenism to citizenship», *Innocenti Essay*, nº 4, Florencia, Unicef.

HILTUS, S. and HART, R. (1994): «Participatory planning and design of recreational spaces with children», *Architecture & Comportement*, 10 (4), pp. 361-370.

HORELLI, L. (1994): «Children as urban planner», *Architecture & Comportement*, 10 (4), pp. 371-377.

LORENZO, R. (1995a): «La città immaginata dai ragazzi», *Paesaggio urbano*, 2, pp. 34 37.

— 1995b «La città dell'infanzia: parole, programmi, partecipazione, ricerche e speriamo progetti concreti», *Paessagio urbano*, 2, pp. 16-21.

MOORE, R. (1978): «Playground at the crossroad?», in ALTMANN, I. and ZUBE, E. H. (editors): *Human behavior and environment*, 10, Public places and space, New York, Plenum Press, pp. 83-127.

NAGY, N. and BAIRD, J. C. (1978): «Children as environmental planners», in ALTMANN, I. and WHOLWILL, J. F. (editors): *Human behavior and environment, 3, Children and environment*, New York, Plenum Press, pp. 259-295.

NICHOLSON, S. (1973): *Community participation in city decision making*, New York, The Open University Press.

— 1975 Children as planners, London, BEE.

Publications of the Italian associations

CONSOLI, V. and TONUCCI, F. (1993): «Ridateci la nostra città», *Quaderno di educazione ambientale*. n° 40, Milan, WWF Italy.

DI GIULIO, A.; QUADRELLI, A. M.; BOSSI, A. and COMANA, F. (1994): «Tutta la mia città», *Quaderno di educazione ambientale*, n° 27, Milan, WWF Italy.

DI GIULIO, A. and QUADRELLI, A. M. M. (1995 *a*): «Circondario», *Quaderno di educazione ambientale ragazzi*, n. 30, Milan, WWF Italy.

— (1995*b*) «Circondario», *Quaderno di educazione ambientale insegnanti*, n°31, Milan, WWF Italy.

FRATODDI, M. and TRABONA, R. (1996): *100 Strade per giocare*, Naples, Cuen.

LORENZO, R. (1988): «Scopriamo l'ambiente urbano», *Quaderno di educazione ambientale*, n° 1, Milan, WWF Italy.

— (1993) *Come riconquistare le nostre città*, Milan, WWF Italy.

PAGLIARINI, C. (1996): *Manuale dei consigli comunali dei ragazzi*, Roma, Democrazia in Erba.

Other cited works

CORZO TORAL, J. L. (1983): *La escritura colectiva: teoría y práctica de la escuela de Barbiana*, Madrid, Anaya.

ESCUELA DE BARBIANA (1970): *Carta a una maestra*, Barcelona, Nova Terra.

LODI, M. (1972): *La mongolfiera*, Milan, Einaudi.

OLIVERIO FERRARIS, A. (1995): *Tu per un figlio*, Bari, Laterza.

PENNAC, D. (1993): *Como una novela*, Barcelona, Anagrama.

RODARI, G. (1979): *Parole per giocare*, Florence, Manzuoli.

— 1979 «Un señor de oreja verde», in TONUCCI, F. (1991) *Con ojos de niño*. Barcelona, Barcanova.

Works by Francesco Tonucci published in Spain:

(1975) La escuela como investigación, Barcelona, Avance.

TONUCCI, F. (Under the direction of); CECCHINI, M (1977): *A los tres años se investiga*, Barcelona, Avance.

(1978) *Por una escuela alternativa*, Barcelona, GUIX.

(1979) Nueva edición ampliada: Barcelona, Reforma de la Escuela.

(1981) *Viaje alrededor de «El Mundo»*, Barcelona, Laia.

RICCI, G. and TONUCCI, F. (1981): *El primer año de nuestro niño*, Barcelona, Reforma de la Escuela.

(1983) *Con ojos de niño*, Barcelona, Barcanova.

(1985) *Niño se nace*, Barcelona, Barcanova.

(1988) Nueva edición: Hogar del Libro, Bar celona.

(1988) *Los materiales*, Vic, Eumo.

(1989) *L'infant i nosaltres*, Vic (Osona), Eumo Editorial (only in Catalan).

(1989) *Cómo ser niño*, Barcelona, Barcanova.

(1990) *¿Enseñar o aprender? la escuela como investigación quince años después*, Barcelona, Editorial Graó.

(1994) *La soledad del niño*, Barcelona, Barcanova.

(1995) *FRATO: Si no os hacéis como yo*, Madrid, PPC.

(1995) *Con ojos de maestro*, Buenos Aires, Troquel

www.ingramcontent.com/pod-product-compliance
Lightning Source LLC
Chambersburg PA
CBHW070429270326
41926CB00014B/2997